GOLF
MINI BOOK

Rich Mintzer

Adams Media Corporation
Holbrook, Massachusetts

Copyright ©2001, Adams Media Corporation.
All rights reserved. This book, or parts thereof, may not be
reproduced in any form without permission from the publisher;
exceptions are made for brief excerpts used in published reviews.

An Everything® Series Book.
"Everything" is a registered trademark of Adams Media Corporation.

Published by Adams Media Corporation
260 Center Street, Holbrook, MA 02343
www.adamsmedia.com

ISBN: 1-58062-500-2

Printed in Canada.

J I H G F E D C B A

Library of Congress Cataloging-in-Publication Data
available from the publisher.

This publication is designed to provide accurate and authoritative information with regard to the subject matter covered. It is sold with the understanding that the publisher is not engaged in rendering legal, accounting, or other professional advice. If legal advice or other expert assistance is required, the services of a competent professional person should be sought.
— From a *Declaration of Principles* jointly adopted by a Committee of the American Bar Association and a Committee of Publishers and Associations

Cover illustrations by Barry Littmann.
Interior illustrations by Barry Littmann.

*This book is available at quantity discounts for bulk purchases.
For information, call 1-800-872-5627.*

Contents

Introduction 5

Hole 1 **7**
Golf History

Hole 2 **45**
The Abridged "Official Rules"

Hole 3 **81**
Golf Etiquette

Hole 4 🏌 **115**

Playing the Game

Hole 5 🏌 **135**

Mental Crosstraining

Hole 6 🏌 **157**

Anecdotes, Quotes, Jokes, and Trivia

Introduction

Once considered the game of the wealthy, thankfully golf has changed its image. Over the past five years, more than 75 percent of the new courses opened in the United States have been for the public. Daily-fee golf has brought the sport to the masses, and many public schools—from grade school through high school—now teach golf. Today, there are over twenty-five million golfers, playing over 15,000 courses. Some play for the challenge of mastering a difficult skill. Others simply enjoy the opportunity to be outside in the fresh air, pitting themselves against nature.

Golf was not always exactly like the game we now know and love. It is thought to have originated in ancient Rome, where it was played with a club and leather ball. Since then it has survived many incarnations and innovations. Even today, as technology has improved, golf continues to evolve. Serious players now use computerized gadgets to measure the speed of their swing or the trajectory of their shot.

But the best thing about golf is that anyone can learn to play. The game is not dependent on technology, strength, or speed—it's a game of strategy. In this new little book we've clearly outlined the basic rules of the game, including proper etiquette for on and off the green. You'll also find expert tips and suggestions that can improve anyone's game, along with loads of fun and interesting historical facts and golf trivia. Whether you're a beginner or a seasoned golfer, this book is packed with information you are sure to enjoy!

Hole 1
Golf History

The origins of the game, not unlike many a modern scorecard, are widely disputed. A host of ancient games resembled golf in some manner, with a club of some sort striking a ball. The Romans played a game called *pagancia,* using a leather ball stuffed with flack. In England a similar game was played in the fourteenth century called *cambuca. Pall mall,* or *jeu de mail,* also involved hitting a ball with a stick and was played by the Italians and later the French in the seventeenth century.

Perhaps the oldest resemblance to golf came from Holland in 1296, where four holes were played in a game that also involved a ball and a stick of some sort. Belgium holds the distinction of creating golf in the form of a game called *chole.* A derivation of hockey, this game was played in Flanders, Belgium, and dates back as far as the 1350s. Many of the oldest games, however, appear from old drawings to be more closely related to hockey, as they involve several players and one ball, and are played in the ice or snow.

Another resemblance to golf came from Scotland, where in the early fifteenth century a newer version of the game of *chole* was introduced. It was this game that, over the next twenty to thirty years, is said to have emerged into what we know as golf.

However golf began it was soon put to a halt, at least in Scotland. Golf, along with football, was banned in the late 1450s in Scotland because it was interfering with archery practice, a key element to military training for the war with England. King James II banned the game, as did James III in the 1470s and James IV in the 1490s. Finally, in 1502 the trend came to an end and the ban was lifted. King James IV then purchased clubs made from a bow maker in Scotland. This purchase of clubs set the stage for golf's return to popularity in Scotland.

In the 1550s the archbishop of St. Andrews issued a decree that gave the locals the okay to play golf on the links at St. Andrews. By 1567, Mary, Queen of Scots, had taken up the game, becoming the first known female golfer.

Golf continued to grow in popularity throughout England and Scotland. In 1618, King James VI even allowed the public to play golf on Sundays. Also around this time a new ball, the feathery, made from two pieces of leather stuffed with boiled feathers, became popular. (The ball would remain in vogue for over 200 years.) Soon links courses started to appear in other parts of Scotland, with holes ranging from 100 yards to a quarter of a mile in distance.

Clubs and Competitions

In 1682, Leith, Scotland, played a role in golf history by hosting the first recorded golf match, which pitted the Duke of York and John Paterstone of Scotland against two English noblemen. The Duke of York brought a man along to carry his clubs for him, the first evidence of a caddie.

Since the game had become a popular pastime throughout Britain and Scotland, it was only fitting that a club be formed strictly for the purpose of golf. Thus the Honourable Company of Edinburgh Golfers was formed. An annual competition was started, with a silver cup given to the winner. The first such winner was a fellow named John Rattray.

Not to be outdone, golfers at St. Andrews in 1754 purchased a silver cup, held an open championship, and gave the cup to the winner, Bailie William Landale. With championship matches becoming fashionable, there arose a need for standardized rules and regulations, so the golfers at St. Andrews printed the first codified rules of golf. By 1760, stroke play became accepted for such tournaments. (Up to that point only match play had been used.)

In 1764, St. Andrews had 11 holes, which when played in both directions equaled a 22-hole course. They decided to combine the first four holes into two, making a 9-hole course, or eighteen when played once out and once back. The golfers at St. Andrews did not realize that their little decision would become the standard for generations to come.

In 1767, a score of 94 by James Durham set the St. Andrews record. That score would stand, amazingly, for the next eighty-six years! Meanwhile, Leith, always competitive with St. Andrews, erected the first golf club house in 1768.

By 1783, Glasgow was among those offering a silver cup for competition winners. In the New World, America requested and received a shipment of 96 clubs and 432 balls from Great Britain in 1743. It was not until 1786, however, that the South Carolina Golf Club was formed in Charleston, the first golf club outside the United Kingdom. The Savannah Club would follow in 1795, but golf would not come to prominence in the United States for another 100 years.

Balls, Books, and Other Breakthroughs

Nearing the middle of the nineteenth century, a major breakthrough in golf equipment made a significant impact on the game. The guttie or gutta percha ball was created and replaced the long-time favorite, the feathery. The ball was less expensive to produce, could be made more quickly, and could fly much farther, adding another twenty to thirty yards to a drive than that of the feathery.

The new ball was made from a rubberlike tree sap that was more resilient than the feathery. Originally, the guttie had a smooth cover, but golfers found that when the cover was nicked or scraped, the ball's aerodynamic properties were changed. This was the start of a myriad of cover patterns that are still emerging today.

Ball Story

The rubber core ball started the new era of ball manufacturing. Between 1902 and 1905 there were ninety-seven patents issued for new balls. There were forty-one during that time period issued in the United States, but none would match Haskell's rubber-core gem. The new ball would turn par fives into par fours, and everyone liked the idea of getting closer to the green.

New developments in golf balls in the era from 1910 to 1915 included:

- A ball with four tiny steel balls inside, fixed in a plain rubber center, surrounded by rubber thread, wound tightly, and covered with composition.
- A ball with four tiny, loose steel balls inside.
- A ball with a rubber core and mercury in the middle.
- An American creation called the pneumatic ball, filled with compressed air and a composition cover. This was originally developed as the Pneu-Matic ball in 1906 and later developed again between 1910–1915 as the pneumatic ball.
- A ball with a center of water.
- A ball with a center of jelly or soft soap.
- A ball filled with an incompressible fluid such as glycerine.

By the 1930s all golf balls had dimples. By the 1960s, 336 manufacturers had produced a variety of patterns, shapes, and sizes to promote a more effective air follow around the ball in flight. The result was greater consistency in flight and ability to design customized trajectories.

In 1856 an important rule change was instituted that said a ball must be played as it lies in match play. Although ignored by many a casual golfer, the rule was an important one that is still part of tournament play.

As golf was beginning its emergence as the world's most popular game, the first of millions of how-to books was published in 1857 by H. B. Farnie called *A Keen Hand*. The top professional golfer of the era was Allen Robertson, while George Condie was regarded as the top amateur by virtue of winning the first Amateur Championship at Perth. Open to both amateurs and professionals, the British Open began its long and storied history in 1861.

Golf in America

As for golf in the United States, it would begin its rise in the 1880s. Early courses included Oakhurst in West Virginia in 1884, the Dorsett Field Club in Vermont in 1886, St. Andrews in Yonkers in 1888, and the Middlesboro Club in 1889. By 1894 there were over seventy golf clubs in America. During the 1890s the first public golf course was opened at Van Courtlandt Park in New York City, and the famed Shinnecock Hills Golf Club was founded, also in New York.

Pretty soon amateur championships were being held at several clubs. Two clubs, in fact, claimed to have the official amateur champion. On December 22, 1894, in an effort to establish a central body with uniform rules and regulations, the United States Golf Association (USGA) was formed. Five clubs would make up the original USGA, including the Chicago Country Club in Wheaton, Illinois; The Country Club in Brookline, Massachusetts; The Newport Golf Club in Newport, Rhode Island; St. Andrews Golf Club in Yonkers, New York; and Shinnecock Hills Golf Club in Southampton, New York.

Now that they had become the official governing body of golf in the United States, the USGA could host national tournaments. Newport Country Club had already staged a twenty player event, which eight players finished, taking four attempts at the course. St. Andrews, in Yonkers, had held their own tournament as well. In 1895, the first official U.S. Open was played in Newport, Rhode Island. Postponed from September to October, so as not to interfere with the yacht races, the championship was won by Horace Rawlings. It was the first of what would become the premier event in American golf for years to come.

Ladies Golf

In the 1890s ladies golf in the British Isles was on the rise. By 1893, the British Isles Golf Union, the first official women's golf organization, had been formed. Margaret Scott won their first Open Championship.

The U.S. Women's amateur event was also decided in 1895. Thirteen ladies played 18 holes at the Meadowbrook Country Club in Hempstead, Long Island. Mrs. Charles S. Brown claimed the first victory with a score of 132. Women's golf had already taken shape in the United States. Just a year after the formation of the women's golf union in the British Isles, the Morris County Club in Morristown, New Jersey had the distinction of being the first club founded entirely by women. The course had cleverly named holes such as Hoodoo, Blasted Hopes, and Sunset.

The Game Grows in the States

Nearing the turn of the century, men, women, and even college students were getting into the act. In 1897 Louis Bayard Jr., won the first ever NCAA Championship. And, if no one knew what was transpiring in the world of golf until that point, they were able to read about it by the end of 1897 when *Golf* magazine was published for the first time.

The keys to the growing success were the advent of new equipment, the popularity of competitions, and the design of many new courses. Golf architect Donald Ross, from Scotland, was one of the premier golf architects of the time, designing over 200 courses,

some of which are still in existence today. Equipment previously imported from Great Britain was now being made primarily in the United States. Hickory for shafts emanated from the Tennessee Hickory Belt, while persimmon and dogwood were also used for club making.

As golf flourished along the East Coast, slightly more inland major technical accomplishments were taking place. Workers at the BF Goodrich Company in Akron, Ohio, adapted the art of winding rubber thread under tension on a solid rubber core. They utilized this newly founded creation to invent the rubber golf ball. The new ball was livelier than the popular

gutta percha ball and could be mass produced more easily. By the year 1900 golf balls could be produced in factories instead of shops. Golf balls became a big industry, and as the equipment became more easily accessible, the number of golfers rose rapidly in the United States.

By 1900, Coburn Haskell patented the rubber-cored ball, which ushered in the modern age of golf and led to standardizing the size and weight of the ball. Within a year, Walter Travis won the U.S. Amateur Open, Sandy Herd won the British Open, and Laurie Auchterlonie won the U.S. Women's Open, all with the Haskell ball. That satisfied doubts of golfers worldwide, and the ball became the standard of the game. The golf ball would evolve over the years thanks to scientific advances. Materials would be added, including balata, surlyn, and lithium. Balls were constructed in one-, two-, and three-piece constructions, but the golf ball designed by Haskell is still basically the same today.

Also at the turn of the century, a dentist in Boston, Doctor George Grant (the first black graduate of the Harvard School of Dentistry) would invent the first wooden golf tee. In upcoming years, American inventors and golfers with extra time on their hands would create over 150 different kinds of tees, including plastic and copper ones. Along with new tees would come new ways to grip a golf club. British golf star Harry Vardon, who had come over on a very successful exhibition tour in 1900 and won the U.S. Open and British Open, would go on to immortality by establishing the overlapping "Vardon" grip, a standard grip for many golfers.

On the equipment front, not to be outdone by American ingenuity, an Englishman, William Taylor, would create the first dimple pattern for golf balls in 1905. Thousands, if not millions, of patterns would emerge over the years since Taylor's original dimpled ball.

As is always the case, when something is made that works someone will try to top it. In 1906, Goodrich decided to market their latest creation, the Pneu-Matic golf ball, a very lively ball featuring a rubber core filled with compressed air. The problem was that in warm weather the ball was prone to explode. This didn't sit well with the golfing community, and production of the ball was stopped.

While the equipment was changing, new courses were coming into play. In 1901, Donald Ross built the first of many Pinehurst Resort courses at the Carolina Hotel, which would become one of the most highly rated resort courses in the world. Two years later, Oakmont, a legendary course designed by Harry Fownes, opened in Oakmont, Pennsylvania. Over the next several years, course building would become a very significant and lucrative endeavor, as hotels and country clubs realized the value of a neighboring golf course.

Tournaments and Champions

As golf continued to grow in popularity, the number of tournaments and prize money also grew. By 1908, Mrs. Gordon Robertson became the first female golfer to turn pro. One year later, the USGA ruled that caddies, caddymasters, and greenskeepers over the age of sixteen were considered professional golfers. That rule would be drastically altered in years to come.

As the equipment evolved and rules were restructured to fit the many new advancements, championship play became more popular. The British golf scene was dominated by John Ball, who won eight consecutive British Amateur Championships. Meanwhile, championships and matches were taking place all over the world, and in 1913 the first international professional match was held between the United States and France.

In 1916, to help organize and standardize the professional golf tournaments popping up at numerous clubs, the PGA of America was formed. The organization had eighty-two charter members, and the first PGA Championship was held in Bronxville, New

York, and won by Jim Barnes. Within a decade, tournaments were being held coast to coast, with Florida, Texas, and California getting into the act.

Just as fast as golf was sweeping the international scene, so was World War I. The First World War soon put the British Open, the U.S. Open and the PGA Championship on hold for several years, and slowed the production of golf equipment, as military equipment became a prime concern.

After the War

By the Roaring Twenties the progress of golf was back on track. The Walker Cup Matches were initiated, and the Olympic Club in San Francisco and Winged Foot in New York were first opened. Both would become landmark golf locales. Courses were now part and parcel of forty-five states across the country.

While courses were opening up from coast to coast, equipment continued to advance with new technology. Changes occurring in equipment between World Wars included the switch from wooden to steel shafts, persimmon and laminated club heads, and deep-grooved irons which were later banned in 1929 by both the USGA and the R&A. Even the U.S. Department of Agriculture got into the swing of golf, developing what is known as creeping bentgrass for putting greens. By this time, American manufacturers of golf equipment were relying more heavily on science and mathematical precision to create matching sets of clubs than on visual judgment and the feel of the club. The USGA and R&A were kept very busy, trying hard not to let any such changes ruin the tradition and integrity of the game.

It was also in the 1920s that golf clubs were no longer referred to by name, and were replaced by the series of numbers still used today. And who was playing with these new "numbered" clubs in this era? The one and only Bobby Jones, a player who would change the face of the game. From 1923 through 1930, Jones won thirteen national championships before retiring from competitive golf in 1930 at the age of only twenty-eight. Jones won everything in sight and heightened the interest in golf as a spectator sport in America. Jones won the U.S. and British Amateurs and the U.S. and British Opens all in one year, one of the most outstanding feats in all of sports history. Perhaps his most significant distinction was his ousting of the British from dominance in the game in America. Until that time British players such as Horace Rawlings, Joe Lloyd, Fred Herd, Willie Smith, and Harry Vardon were the stars of the game.

The battle between the United States and Great Britain would heat up and a biennial tournament would be initiated in 1927 to decide the champion. Billed as the United States versus Europe, the Ryder Cup got under way, with Walter Hagen captaining the American team for the first seven years. The United States would go on to dominate the Ryder Cup with captains that would include Jack Nicklaus, Arnold Palmer, and Sam Snead.

As the Depression grew near, golf clubs were still springing up, most notably at Cypress Point in California and in Palm Beach, Florida, where the Seminole Golf Club first opened its doors. Out west, the Los Angeles Country Club staged the first L.A. Open, the third-oldest PGA tournament still in existence today. They offered a $10,000 purse, which at that time was equivalent to the purses of today's tournaments.

Through the '30s the PGA saw the tour money rise to over $130,000, and sponsors like Hershey Chocolate began their association with the tour. Celebrities soon became part of the golf scene, as the Bing Crosby Pro-Am kicked off in 1937 in San Diego. In 1938 charities linked up with golf as well, with the Palm Beach Invitational becoming the first tournament to make a major charitable contribution of $10,000.

The Masters and the War Begin

In 1934, Bobby Jones began a little tournament for a few of his friends. The tournament would evolve into the Masters Tournament, one of the most prestigious of the game. Jones played in the first several as a courtesy to his guests. Unlike many tournaments that would find new homes every year, the Masters would remain in Augusta, Georgia.

Just as the USGA ruled a limit of fourteen clubs per golfer, equipment production was once again slowed to a halt. World War II reared its ugly head, and many PGA touring pros found themselves joining the military. Major tournaments were halted as the world focused on the events in Europe.

In the years following the war, golf found itself back on track rather quickly. The first U.S. Women's Open was played, and was won by Patty Berg. Golf was first seen on local television, as the U.S. Open was broadcast in St. Louis. There were no slow-motion, stop-action replays of every swing, but bringing the game to television increased golf's popularity.

In 1950 the Women's Professional Golf Association was replaced by the Ladies

Professional Golf Association (LPGA), beginning a new rise to prominence of women's golf in America. Patty Berg was the initial president, and by 1952 there were twenty-one tournaments on the LPGA tour. Besides Patty, who split her time between the LPGA administrative work and her own successful career, other top women golfers of the early '50s including Babe Zaharias, Marilyn Smith, Peggy Kirk, Louise Suggs, and Betsy Rawls established a first-rate core of lady professional golfers.

Meanwhile on the men's tour, players like Byron Nelson, Bobby Locke, and Ben Hogan were among the giants of the sport, while Al Brosch shot a 60 at the Texas Open to set a new PGA record in 1951.

Throughout the 1950s more and more people were becoming interested in the game. Magazines and books were regularly keeping the public in touch with what the pros were doing and included tips on how to play. The game was not only for country clubbers, but was promoted for all to enjoy. In fact, Tommy Armour's *How to Play Your Best Golf* became the first golf book to make the bestseller list. In 1954 the U.S. Open was televised nationally for the first time, followed in 1956 by the Masters and in 1957 by the weekly series called *All Star Golf.*

The 1960s saw tremendous growth in the popularity of PGA events and ushered in the era of Arnold Palmer. Palmer would win the 1960 Masters and U.S. Open, and the 1961

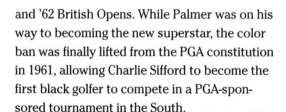

and '62 British Opens. While Palmer was on his way to becoming the new superstar, the color ban was finally lifted from the PGA constitution in 1961, allowing Charlie Sifford to become the first black golfer to compete in a PGA-sponsored tournament in the South.

Elsewhere, Gary Player would become the first foreign-born player to win the Masters, and some kid named Nicklaus would break into the professional ranks in 1962, notching his first professional win at the U.S. Open. Meanwhile, by 1965 Sam Snead would amass an incredible eighty-one tour victories. There was a growing interest in becoming a professional golfer, and for the many professional hopefuls the PGA set up their qualifying school at the National Golf Club in Palm Beach Gardens.

By the start of the '60s the LPGA tour money reached $200,000, and in 1963 the LPGA made it to television with the U.S.

Women's Open Championship. It was also in the early '60s that Kathy Whitworth embarked on the first stretch of what would amount to an incredible eighty-eight LPGA titles.

Throughout the decade the LPGA continued growing in stature and received more coverage by the sports media. A Hall of Fame was established, and by the end of the '60s, prize money was up to $600,000 in a total of thirty-four tournaments.

As the '60s unfolded, professional and amateur golfers set a host of astounding new records. Bill Burke shot an amazing 57 at Normandie Country Club, a new low for an 18-hole course. Arnold Palmer won the 1965 Masters with a record 271, and three years later became the first player to surpass $1 million in career PGA earnings. An amateur golfer named Norman Manley became the first player to score consecutive holes-in-one on par-four holes at the Del Valley Country Club. But as if all the excitement of golf around the world wasn't enough, Alan Shepard would round out the '60s by hitting two legendary shots with a 6-iron on a course called Fra Mauro Country Club, not a country club at all, but actually a little place on the moon.

Back on Earth

As the '70s progressed, so did the game. The graphite shaft was invented; Lee Elders became the first black golfer in the Masters; and Jack Nicklaus won his fourteenth major PGA championship to surpass Bobby Jones. By the mid-1970s the PGA was indeed a profitable big business, with total revenues of nearly $4 million. Lee Trevino, Hale Irwin, Tom Watson, and Johnny

Miller rose to prominence in the sport, and the number of tournaments grew steadily, as did the number of sponsors and purses. In 1978 the first Legends of Golf was played in Austin, Texas, and would become the precursor to the PGA-sanctioned Senior Tour. Judy Rankin became the first LPGA golfer to surpass $100,000 in income in one season, and Nancy Lopez won five tournaments in a row.

The '80s offered a whole new type of club. Golf's first oxymoron came in the form of metal woods introduced by a company called Taylor Made. Back on the spectator scene, the Players Club at Sawgrass opened and became the prototype for other "stadium" courses, designed to allow greater visibility for spectators. Despite the lack of vendors hawking peanuts, popcorn, and golf tees, the stadium courses were a major success. While spectators were getting a closer, better look at the action, golfers who kept playing into their 50s, 60s, and beyond now had the Senior Tour, which was introduced by the PGA with two events.

On the women's circuit, Kathy Whitworth became the first female golfer to surpass $1 million in career earnings. Tour money was over $4 million, and in 1982 the entire four rounds of the Nabisco Dinah Shore tournament was televised. Pretty soon, the number of lady golfers trying to become professionals would have the LPGA incorporating an all-exempt qualifying system. Corporate sponsorship now became a staple of women's golf, and the prize money and number of tournaments continued to grow. Beth Daniel, Betsy King, and Patty Sheehan were among the pros leading the way.

In the '80s, money in sports began to take off dramatically. In 1986 the Panasonic Las Vegas International offered the first $1 million purse. By 1988 Curtis Strange became the first golfer to exceed the $1 million mark in one season, and thirty players competed for a $2 million purse in the first Nabisco Championship, which would later become the Tour Championship. As the purse money and player earnings grew, so did the charitable contributions by the PGA and LPGA, which exceeded $200 million in the 1980s alone.

As the '80s wound to a fruitful conclusion for the LPGA, prize money topped $14 million, and the LPGA Urban Youth Golf Program and LPGA Girls Golf Club were established to fortify programs for girls interested in golf.

As the '90s ushered in the era of astounding (even obscene) money in professional sports, the Shadow Creek Golf Club hired Tom Fazio to design a course in the Las Vegas desert that would cost somewhere in the area of $50 million. *Golf Digest* ranked the course in their top ten in 1994, outraging those who didn't like the idea that money could buy you a highly rated course.

The 1990s also sparked more and more tournaments, as companies from coast to coast vied to sponsor a golf championship event of some type. The PGA-sanctioned Nike Tour, which began in the early '90s as the Hogan Tour; the Futures Tour for women; the U.S. Golf Tour; and others were establishing a training ground for the future professionals. On the professional front, the LPGA initiated a Ryder Cup tournament of its own, the Solheim Cup, a biennial event pitting the United States against Europe, and between 1990 and 1995, the PGA donated over $130 million to charity.

As always, new and inventive equipment continued to appear on the golf scene, then in the form of oversized metal woods. The clubs sold like hotcakes, as golfers were enthusiastic about their better chance to find the sweet spot.

By the mid-1990s golf was all over the place. Companies routinely held golf outings for their clients and offered incentive golf packages for their best employees; golf tours took travelers across Europe and Asia; and an all-golf channel debuted on cable, providing twenty-four hours of golf information. Super stores sold golf equipment at an astounding rate; golf courses covered what were once landfills; and nearly all PGA and LPGA tournaments were covered on television. By 1995 there were over 25 million golfers in America, playing nearly 500 million rounds of golf a year. WOW!

Then in 1996 and 1997, Tiger Woods gave golf another giant shot in the arm. The young phenom won four of his first 12 events as a professional, including the 1997 Masters. He went on to win his last five tournaments of the decade and eight for the year, including the 1999 PGA Championship. He also garnered PGA Player of the Year honors. In 2000, Woods won nine more tournaments, and became the youngest player ever to win a career Grand Slam.

The turn of this century also saw young Ernie Els become one of the fastest rising players on the PGA tour. He finished second to Woods in six tournaments, and won a few as well. Tragic news shook the golf world as one of the game's most popular players, Payne Stewart, died in a plane crash at the end of 1999.

The LPGA celebrated the start of the new millennium with its 50th anniversary. From 1950, when the LPGA began with 14 tournaments and $50,000 in prizes, the tour has grown to 42 events, and $38 million in prize money. LPGA star Se Ri Pak of Korea came off her Rookie of the Year status in 1998 with eight tour victories, and won some $2 million in the first six months of the new century.

The next century of golf welcomes a host of new technology, as clubmakers and ball manufacturers try all sorts of metals and designs to further defy the laws of physics. Meanwhile, audiences enjoy more golf on television and there is a wealth of top-notch computer golf games for all to play. However, nothing replaces the real thing, and golfers continue to hit the links in record numbers in 2001.

Hole 2

The Abridged "Official Rules"

Until 1951, the United States Golf Association (USGA) and the Royal and Ancient Golf Club (R&A) of St. Andrews, Scotland, governed the rules of golf as separate entities. Each had a somewhat strained relationship with the other. Fortunately, for our sake, the USGA and the R&A now work closely together to refine and govern the rules of the game. The rules of golf are updated by the USGA every year and are decided by a committee of four to fourteen people who serve for two years.

Golf's Most Common Rules

The USGA publishes a 144-page book entitled *Rules of Golf,* and to reproduce it here would be akin to trying to play all eight Pinehurst courses in one day. The USGA also publishes a six-panel card entitled "Golf Rules in Brief." It is from that publication that we have adapted most of the rules in this section.

Some of the rules discussed distinguish between match play and stroke play. Match play is a game for twosomes where each hole is a separate contest within the round. The player with the most holes won in this type of game wins the *match.* Stroke play (also known

as medal play) is individual play. Here, the player with the lowest score for the entire round wins.

It should be understood that the following adaptation is designed to explain some of golf's most common rules and is not sanctioned by the USGA. This is strictly the author's adaptation. So without further ado, here's the dirt, or should we say the divot, on golf's adherent guidelines.

Before Teeing Off

Make sure your ball is identified with some sort of marking. If you can't identify your ball during play and you discover that someone in your group has an identical ball, then your ball is considered lost and that means you lose a stroke. See the Dropping In section later in this chapter.

You or your caddie are allowed to carry between one and fourteen clubs on the course. If you go for the maximum, have your chiropractor's number handy.

In the "Hey, what's that?" category, you may not use an artificial device or unusual equipment to measure distance or conditions. Leave your binoculars at home. If you are unsure what is considered artificial or unusual, contact the USGA.

Gripping

When gripping the club, plain gloves may be worn. Resin or drying powders may be used too, as well as a moisturizing lotion if you desire. Tape, gauze, even a towel may be applied to the grip to help your stroke, as long as the grip itself isn't specifically molded for your hands.

Advice

As far as advice goes, keep in mind that everyone plays differently and advice is rarely appreciated unless a pro is giving it to a player who is taking a lesson. During a game, the only person you can ask advice from is your partner or your caddie. That goes for giving advice too.

Practice Swings and Strokes

Practice swings are allowed, but not practice strokes. You can't hit the ball and then exclaim, "That was just practice!" While playing you may take as many practice swings as you want. Keep the game moving; one must play without delay. Any excessive delay in play (overdoing the practice swings, crying, etc.) is considered a delay of the game and incurs a penalty stroke.

Ready to Play

On the first tee, the players draw (or determine by lot if a draw is not available) to decide the order of the participants.

Place your tee within two club lengths behind the front edges of the tee markings. If you tee off outside this area during match play, the opposition may, and rightly so, ask you to replay the stroke. If you do this during stroke play, you are penalized two strokes and then must play within the proper tee settings. In other words, this is not the place for creativity.

During a *match,* after teeing off, the ball farthest from the hole is played first. When the next hole is ready to be played, the winner of the previous hole tees off first. If a player for any reason plays out of place anywhere through the course, opponents can rightfully ask this individual to replay the stroke.

During *stroke* play after teeing off, the ball farthest from the hole is played first. The player with the lowest score of the previous hole tees off from the next hole first. In the event of a tie on the hole, the honor for the next tee goes to the player who teed off on the previous hole. Note that in stroke play playing out of turn is generally not penalized.

Now That We're in Play

Strike the ball from where it has landed, or as it's generally known, where the ball lies. For the most part, you are not allowed to move the ball without incurring a penalty stroke unless a rule permits so. You are allowed to move the ball without penalty if it lands in casual water (golfspeak for puddle). The same goes if another player has inadvertently moved your ball. Here, no penalty is incurred if you place the ball back in its original spot.

You are not allowed to improve your lie while on the fairway. If you find your ball in a spot where your swing is interrupted by a tree branch, you may not alter this object in any way. Nor may you press anything down. You may remove an object if it interferes with your stance, but only if that object is removable (i.e., don't ask the greenskeeper for explosives to remove this annoyance). If your ball lies in a bunker or water hazard, you are not permitted to touch the ground in the bunker or water hazard before the downswing.

A ball is to be struck with the clubhead. Pushing it or scraping it is not considered striking the ball. If your club hits the ball more than once in a single swing, that stroke is counted plus a penalty stroke.

In match play, if you strike the wrong ball you lose the hole. If this occurs in stroke play, add on a two-stroke penalty and then play the correct ball.

The Proof Is in the Putting

Once on the green, lift the ball and place a marker where it lies. During this time you may clean the ball or replace it. It is your turn to putt when your ball is farther away from the cup. If you putt the ball and it does not drop into the cup and other players are farther out than you are, lift your ball again and mark its lie until it's your turn to putt again. Keep in mind that the only time your ball should be on the green is when it's your turn to putt.

Pressing anything down in the line of your ball to the hole is not permitted. However, if there is an old hole mark/plug in the line of putt, you may repair it. Removal of objects in the line of the putt is also allowed by using your hand or your golf club. Using a leaf blower would be a tad overdoing it. Testing the surface of the green by scraping or rolling the ball on its surface is not permitted.

In match play, if all the players are now on the green and for some odd reason your ball strikes the flagstick, you lose the hole. In stroke play, if you hit the flagstick, you incur a two-stroke penalty. So, pull the flag out of the cup, and place it far away from the hole.

In match play, the ball must be played until the player sinks it, unless the competition acknowledges that the putt could be made, allowing the player to move on to the next tee. Every player must hole out in stroke play. No conceding of strokes is allowed.

The Roving Ball

Whether accidental or not, if your ball is moved by you, your partner, or your caddie, or if it moves after addressing it (you're already in your stance and ready to strike the ball), you must add a penalty stroke and replace the ball where it was. If the ball was moved by anyone else, restore the ball to its original site without penalty. There is also a penalty for moving a ball when searching for a covered ball in a hazard or casual water.

In match play, if your ball is moving and it's stopped by you, your partner, or your caddie in any manner, you lose the hole. During stroke play you are penalized two strokes and the ball is played where it landed.

If your ball is in motion and it's stopped by someone else, play the ball where it lands without penalty to you. In match play if your competition or his caddie has interfered with the ball, you can play the ball where it has rested or replay it. If you're playing a stroke game and you're on the green and the ball is deflected by someone other than yourself or your caddie, you need to play the ball again.

If your ball is moving and is stopped in any manner by another ball in play or at rest, play your ball where it lands. During a match, the player is not penalized. In a stroke game, you are penalized two strokes if your ball and the other ball were on the green before your swing.

Dropping In

Any time a ball is lifted its position needs to be marked and the ball must be replaced. Some of the reasons for dropping are when a ball is lost, lands in water, or is hit out of bounds, or when a player declares his lie unplayable. To drop a ball in play in the fairway, put the ball in your hand, stand straight up and hold the ball out to your side at shoulder height, then drop the ball. If you are dropping a ball that was in a hazard, it must be dropped back into the same hazard, otherwise you lose an additional stroke. If you drop a ball and it hits a player, his partner, a caddie, or any equipment, the ball needs to be redropped. No penalty is incurred, just wrath.

If a dropped ball rolls in, or in and out, of a hazard, finds its way onto the putting green, winds up out of bounds, or is in a position where it is interfered with, the ball must be redropped. Interference includes obstructions, abnormal ground conditions, or an embedded ball. A ball also must be redropped if it lands more than two club lengths from its originally marked spot. If the redropped ball lands in any of the spots mentioned above, replace it where it originally struck the part of the course when it was redropped. *Note:* A redropped ball cannot lie closer to the hole from where it was removed.

Interference

Interference occurs in a myriad of places on the links. If your ball is in the way of another player, you may lift it if it will assist that player. Consequently, you may request that any ball interfering with your play be temporarily removed so that you may continue.

Any natural loose impediments such as rocks, stones, and leaves that are not a solid part of the course but are interfering with your play may be removed. However, if your ball is touching a loose impediment, you must play it as it is. If you move a loose impediment within a club length of your ball and your ball moves, unless it was on the putting green, you must put the ball back in the same spot and receive a penalty stroke.

Obstructions

Unlike interference, an obstruction is a man-made object. However, objects such as fences, stakes, or immovable man-made articles displaying out-of-bounds lines are not considered obstructions.

Obstructions that are movable may be moved. If your ball moves while you move this obstruction you can replace it without being penalized. If you're on the green, you may move any obstructions that are in your ball's line.

Aside from your ball being in a water hazard, you may drop your ball a club length away from an immovable obstruction that blocks your stance or swing. Again, if your ball is in a bunker, you've got to drop it in the bunker. As always, when dropping a ball, you cannot drop it closer to the hole. A lost ball due to an immovable obstruction (this does not include a water hazard) may be replaced at the point where the ball disappeared without penalty.

Unusual Course Conditions

If your ball winds up in casual water or in the midst of ground being repaired, or a strangely possessive animal has run away with it, you may drop a ball without penalty within one club length of the closest point of relief not closer to the hole. If a club length isn't good enough, you may drop a ball in a place closest to the point where it was lost and where you can take a full swing. Under penalty of one stroke, you may drop the ball behind a water hazard and take the shot again. If you're on the putting green, place the ball in the nearest position that allows you a full stroke without interference. And no, you cannot place it closer to the hole.

If your ball is lost under abnormal ground conditions (except for the possessive animal or a water hazard), you may drop the ball at the point where the ball crossed into that area and that allows you a full swing.

Water

If your ball encounters water that isn't so casual (you've given it a bath via a small lake known on the course as a water hazard), you may drop the ball anywhere behind the water hazard as long as it is in line with where the ball took a dive without its scuba gear. You may also replay the shot, or drop the ball on the other side of the water hazard in line with where the ball took a drink. Of course, there's a one-stroke penalty for all of the above.

Provisional Play

Your ball is out of bounds or lying at the bottom of an artificial lake whose beauty you had until recently admired. It is simply lost. At this point you may take a provisional stroke, but only after you've asked in a polite but not pleading way to do so. If the other players agree, drop the ball where you believe the ball was last seen and swing away.

You must, of course, take a penalty stroke for this. If by chance your original ball is found after you've taken the provisional stroke, you must play the original ball and disallow the previous stroke and penalty.

Mission: Impossible

There are those occasions where a ball simply is not playable due to a myriad of situations. In this case, you may drop the ball within two club lengths, but not closer to the hole, and play it from there. You may, if you desire, play the ball again from its original spot. Is there a one-stroke penalty for any of this? You bet. Let's face it, this is a game that can make even the most stolid person whine.

Popular Golf Games and Their Rules
Blind Bogey

In this game, each player does his or her best to come closest to a score that has been pulled out of a hat. Try not to get carried away with this, however. If none of the players scratch (shoot par), don't place the number 68 in the bowl. Start with higher numbers.

Chapman (Similar to Pinehurst)

Each player on a two-person team hits a tee shot. They then each play a second shot using their partner's ball. At this point, they select the best ball, and the player who did not hit plays, alternating shots until the ball is holed.

Four Ball

In this game the better ball of two players is played against the better ball of the two players who oppose them.

Medal Play

This game is used on the PGA tour and is for any number of players. The lowest score for the round wins. This game can also involve Nassau bets. If the abilities of the players vary, handicaps should be incorporated.

Nassau

This is a very popular game for twosomes and foursomes. The Nassau format can be either match or medal play. A $3 Nassau is in reality three bets: one for the front nine, one for the back nine, and one for the entire eighteen holes. Each bet is $3. Foursomes playing Nassau actually would be two-person teams playing a best-ball format in match or medal play. However, most Nassau games are played in the match-play format.

Odd/Even (Also Called Foursomes)

Here, two players play one ball and alternate hitting shots. One player tees off at the odd-numbered holes and the other at the even-numbered holes.

Pinehurst

Similar to Chapman, each player drives a ball from the tee and the players alternate from there until the ball is holed. In Chapman, both players hit each other's second shot and then alternate till the ball is holed.

Round Robin

This is a great game for four players whose abilities vary. Two-person teams play a low ball or a low total game to ascertain the winning team of each hole. During the game you change partners every 6 holes, so by the end of the round, everyone's been paired once. Because partners switch every six holes, you can have three separate bets.

Scotch Foursome

This game has partners who alternate hitting the same ball. This scenario continues on to the next tee regardless of who sank the previous hole's putt.

Scramble

Used for many tournaments, the players, usually a team of four, tee off at the hole as they normally would. After the initial tee off, the team decides which is the best-hit ball and everyone on the team plays from that place. This repeats for each shot until a ball is holed.

Skins

Here's a game for three or more players. A specific bet is agreed upon for each hole (usually all holes are the same amount). The lowest score on each hole wins a designated bet. If a hole is tied for the low score, the bet for that hole is carried over to the next hole. If a player wins the next hole and it includes a carryover, that player wins two skins. If several holes in a row are tied, the value of the next skin increases accordingly. If two players tie, everyone ties. This allows any player to win the next skin regardless of how a player performed on the previous hole.

Threesome

A game where two players in a threesome play the same ball, alternating strokes between them, while the single player plays against them.

Determining Your Handicap

The USGA Handicap System is well recognized and widely accepted by golf clubs throughout the country. This handicap system is based on the best ten differentials from a player's last twenty scores.

A differential is determined by subtracting the USGA Course Rating from the adjusted gross score, then multiplying the resulting value by 113, then dividing this result by the corresponding USGA Slope Rating and rounding off to the nearest tenth.

The following information will help you determine your handicap.

Yardage Rating

"Yardage Rating" is the evaluation of the playing difficulty based on yardage only. It is the score a scratch player on his game is expected to make when playing a course of average difficulty.

USGA Course Rating

"Course Rating" is the evaluation of the playing difficulty of a course for scratch players. Course rating is expressed in strokes and decimal fractions of a stroke, and based on yardage and other obstacles to the extent that they affect the scoring ability of a scratch player.

Courses are rated by authorized golf associations, not by individual clubs.

USGA Slope Rating

"Slope Rating" reflects the relative playing difficulty of a course for players with handicaps above scratch. The lowest Slope Rating is 55 and the highest is 155. The average Slope Rating for men and women is 113.

When not everyone has a USGA handicap, here are three ideas to help handicap the unhandicapped:

Second Best Score System

The USGA has developed a simple estimator of a player's ability called the "Second Best Score System" or "Second Best Handicap" for short. Second Best Handicap is not a substitute for the USGA Handicap System, but it can produce acceptable results and is a reasonable system for handicapping those without handicaps.

To create a player's Second Best Handicap, the tournament committee simply asks each unhandicapped player to submit his or her last three best scores made on a regulation course (par 68 or more) in the last twelve months. They combine these scores with any previous scores the player has made in their tournament in the past two years.

The player's Second Best Handicap is the second best score he or she has given them minus 70 for men and 73 for women.

For example, if a male player submits scores of 92, 96, and 98, and he had a score of 90 in their tournament last year, his second best score would be the 92, and they would subtract 70.

There is a special qualification for beginners or players who can submit only one score. They subtract 74 from the score for a man and 77 for a woman's Second Best Handicap.

If necessary, 9-hole scores can be combined to produce an 18-hole scoring history.

If a player has never played, the Second Best Handicap is not appropriate. The committee should assign a maximum of 36 strokes for men and 40 for women. Some allow a maximum of 50 strokes, which generally gives three strokes on each hole except for par threes.

Modified Peoria System

Another alternative is to use a hole-score selection system called the "Peoria System." Under this system, a player learns his or her handicap after the round is completed. The committee secretly selects a par-three hole, a par-five hole and four par-four holes from an 18-hole course. The par fours should be representative in length and difficulty with two chosen from the front nine and two from the back nine.

A modified Peoria handicap is then calculated by adding the player's strokes over par on the six selected holes and multiplying that number by 2.8. This will be the player's allowance, to be deducted from his or her gross score. The maximum hole score for allowance purposes is three over par on par threes and fours, and four over par on par fives.

Example: A player scores 98 for a round. She is 11 over par on the six selected holes. 11 x 2.8 = 30.8 = 31 allowance. Her net score is, therefore, 98 – 31, or 67.

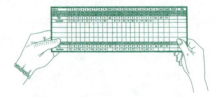

The Scheid System

The Scheid System is a "worst-holes" system for large, unhandicapped events that is designed to give all golfers an equal chance, with a range up to 151. The following table explains it.

The Scheid System

SCORE	DEDUCT
72, 73	no holes and adjustment
74, 75, 76	1/2 worst hole and adjustment
77, 78, 79	1 worst hole and adjustment
80, 81, 82, 83	1 1/2 worst holes and adjustment
84, 85, 86, 87	2 worst holes and adjustment
88, 89, 90, 91	2 1/2 worst holes and adjustment
92, 93, 94, 95	3 worst holes and adjustment
96, 97, 98, 99	3 1/2 worst holes and adjustment
100, 101, 102, 103, 104	4 worst holes and adjustment
105, 106, 107	4 1/2 worst holes and adjustment
110, 111, 112, 113, 114	5 worst holes and adjustment
115, 116, 117, 118, 119, 120	5 1/2 worst holes and adjustment
121, 122, 123, 124, 125, 126	6 worst holes and adjustment
127, 128, 129, 130, 131, 132	6 1/2 worst holes and adjustment
133, 134, 135, 136, 137, 138	7 worst holes and adjustment
139, 140, 141, 142, 143, 144	7 1/2 worst holes and adjustment
145, 146, 147, 148, 149, 150, 151	8 worst holes and adjustment

Adjustment to deduction
−3, −2, −1, 0, +1, +2, +3

The USGA

According to the latest estimations, there are 25 million golfers in the United States and every one of them owes it to themselves to visit the USGA Headquarters and Museum. Located in the sweeping hills in the middle of New Jersey, it has the largest public collection of golf art, memorabilia, and books in the world.

A favorite for visitors is the most unique golf club ever used by any earthling—the club used on the moon by Alan Shepard on his Apollo 14 mission. This amazing display has been recently upgraded and includes footage from NASA showing Shepard swinging away.

There's also a room solely dedicated to Bobby Jones that includes many of his trophies and personal items in a warm, welcoming setting, reminiscent of the era in which he was a champion. Upstairs there's a time-line display showing the beginnings of the game

and how it evolved from a man hitting a ball with a stick to the present-day game. Check out the featheries and gutta perchas.

The library at the museum stocks several thousands of books relating to golf. There's also a gift shop where you can purchase quality clothing and memorabilia, including quality items for the U.S. Open, a tournament the USGA conducts along with the Women's and Senior's Opens.

The main function of the USGA is to uphold the traditions of the game and, with the Royal and Ancient Golf Club in Scotland, to write and interpret the rules of golf.

The USGA has its own Testing Center stocked with state-of-the-art scientific-research technology to test golf clubs and balls for accuracy and conformity to the standards set forth under USGA rules and regulations. The USGA started making equipment rulings as far back as 1908 and has records that go back as far as 1934. They have about 9,000 clubs, which they have ruled upon, in the basement, under lock and key.

Having modernized, the USGA now keeps a detailed computer listing just in case anyone wants to know about the eligibility of a club. A golfer is welcome to call and give them the product name, the company name, and the description, and the USGA will let them know if it is an acceptable club.

Balls cannot exceed 1.68 inches in diameter, weigh less than 1.62 ounces, fly further than 280 yards (plus a 6 percent test tolerance on the USGA range), and go faster than 255 feet per second. Laser beams placed at several points on the ball's path are used to analyze a golf ball's spin rate, launch angle, and velocity.

The lab also analyzes clubhead mechanics, shaft mechanics, impact, and biomechanics (the role the golf swing plays), and has an area devoted to growing and testing grass and sod.

The USGA, however, does not publicize their findings. "It's all confidential information," explains research expert John Mutch. "Manufacturers submit their products . . . they spend a lot of money on research and development and we keep everything confidential. We communicate with the person who submitted it." If the balls conform, the USGA does list them in their conforming golf-ball booklet, which is published twice annually. Manufacturers can either put the balls on a three-year list or a five-year list, whichever they prefer. Only balls in that book can be used, as a condition of play. The U.S. Open, all the USGA events, PGA Tour events, and most club events follow the conditions adhered to in the book.

Anyone can become a member of the USGA and support the great game of golf on all fronts. Membership includes a monthly subscription to the *Golf Journal*, substantial discounts at the gift shop and from the catalog, and a copy of the *Rules of Golf*. Memberships start at a very reasonable $25. Higher membership rates include tickets to the U.S. Open.

> The United States Golf Association
> Headquarters and Museum
> Far Hills, NJ 07931
> 1-800-345-USGA
> *www.usga.org*

Hole 3

Golf Etiquette

Etiquette and integrity are at the very heart of golf. As with the rules, there is enough golf etiquette to fill a book—and such books have been written. You'll discover that most golfing etiquette addresses slow play, the most common complaint from golfers. If every golfer practiced proper etiquette on the course, slow play would be virtually eliminated. Etiquette separates the knowledgeable from the rank amateur.

Generally, etiquette is what you *should* or *should not* do, while the rules are what you *shall* or *shall not* do. Here are some highlights of golf protocol:

Etiquette on Etiquette

If someone in your group is not familiar with golf etiquette, teach them. It will benefit both your game and that person, and help the game move faster.

Fore!

Probably the most considerate thing you can do during a round is to yell "Fore!" A dimpled projectile traveling at over a hundred miles an hour can really do some damage to muscles, bones, and eyes. If you hear this utterance expelled from someone's lungs, proper etiquette is to take cover as best you can. Most choose to hit the deck.

Communication Devices

Avoid bringing beepers, pagers, or cellular phones onto the golf course. If you must do so, turn them off while on the course. Also, if your watch beeps, remember to turn it off at the starter's desk. Having these things go off whether accidentally or intentionally when a player is swinging is considered very rude. You may find yourself talking on the phone and not be aware that you are within earshot of the person currently playing. Enjoy the course and the scenery; let the office survive without you.

Moving Right Along

As previously stated in the rules, golfers are obligated to keep the game moving. Play without delay. Once all the players have sunk their putts, place the flag in the cup, and move on quickly.

It Went That'a Way

Watch your playing partners hit the ball. This way you can help them locate it if need be. This too results in faster play. Also, do not look for your ball or someone else's ball for more than three minutes.

Clothing at the Club

If you're going to a club, call ahead to find out what the dress code is. Generally tee-shirts or halters are not allowed on the grounds. If you're not sure of the dress code, a collared shirt is always appropriate.

- HAT: ONLY IN SCOTLAND
- SHIRT: GOOD
- BELT: TOO MUCH BUCKLE
- WATCH: WEIGHT IMPEDES THE SWING
- GLOVE: NO PROBLEM
- SLACKS: AN OVERSTATEMENT
- FOOTWEAR: ONLY IF YOU PLAN TO SPEND A LOT OF TIME IN THE SAND

Some golf clubs don't allow shorts either, so pants are always appropriate.

No Shirt, No Service

Men, no matter how hot it gets on the course, you should never remove your shirt. Ladies, avoid this too.

Oh, You Kids

If small children are accompanying you out on the course, that's fine. However, make sure that a chaperon accompanies them. Children, being who they are, can interfere with many a golfer's game.

Cheating

Cheating is very easy to do during a golf game. One can write down a 5 on the scorecard instead of a 6, or move the ball to improve the lie without recording a penalty stroke. However, there are times when someone cheats without knowing it. With all the rules golf has, it's no wonder. If you spot someone cheating, whether intentionally or not, the best thing to do is take care of it right there. Needless to say, you should handle this with your most diplomatic balm. Politely informing a player of their infraction at the time of its occurrence gives the player an opportunity to correct his or her temporary lapse.

Pregame
Arranging a Tee Time

To reserve a tee time, call the golf course or golf club in advance of your game. Many players call very early in the week to set up a tee time for the weekend. If you don't get through, don't be discouraged, keep hitting that redial button on your phone.

Once you've made the tee time, if for some reason you cannot arrive at the time you've designated, call the Starter at the course and cancel. This saves a lot of aggravation for the Starter and your fellow golfers waiting to play. This is more than etiquette, it's simply common sense and good faith.

Many golfers who play on a regular basis pay an annual fee to a golf course or club and automatically have a specific tee time reserved for them on a particular day during the week. If for some reason they are unable to make this tee time, they need to cancel or they'll be charged an additional fee. Often golfers will cancel, therefore opening up a time for someone calling in who wants to shoot a round. Arrive at the course roughly half an hour before the tee time you've requested.

Timing

Arrive at the course on time. Tee times are tight. Don't hold up the rest of your two-, three- or foursome. If for some reason a partner is late, notify the starter so he/she can adjust the tee-off times.

It's Time to Change

At most clubs, locker-room facilities are available. If you need to change any clothing before playing, do it there. Even if you're only changing shoes, please do it in the locker room, not in the parking lot or on the course.

Bag the Pro Shop

If you bring your clubs/golf bag into the pro shop, unforced Jerry Lewis–type errors

await you. If you do bring your bag into the shop, the salesperson will make it loud and clear to you to remove the bag from the premises. Park your bag in the area allotted for bags before you venture inside.

Up in Smoke

If you need to smoke out on the links, ask your playing partners if it's okay to light up. Most of the time they'll say it's fine with them. It's simply good form to ask first. Also, remember to keep the course clean. Do not leave cigarette butts on the grounds, and refrain from putting them out on the green.

At the Tee
Greetings

Be the first to step up and introduce yourself to new playing partners.

Who Goes First?

In friendly play off the first tee, decide amongst yourselves the order of play. If ladies are playing in a mixed group, they should be asked to play first. For more serious play you may draw straws. Some prefer to flip a tee. Proceed by throwing a tee in the air and let it land inside the circle of the players. Whoever the tee is pointing to is out. For instance, if you're playing with a foursome and the tee is flipped, whoever it points to first becomes the last to tee off; when the tee is flipped again, whoever the tee is pointing to is out again, and they become the third person to tee off, etc.

Sometimes after players have teed off they stare and moan at the ball they've hit. It is not necessary to wait for them to get out of the box. Have a tee in your hand and step up. It is not rude to do so even if you're out of order. This action also lets the player know that they're slowing things up and that they should be aware of their behavior. Remember, the game is not to be rushed, but it is to be played in a timely fashion.

Which Tee Marker Is for You?

Tee markings allow golfers of different abilities to play together. It is quite common for golfers in the same group to play from different tees. Players should use the tee most suitable to them. If you're a beginner, tee off from the tee marking that's closer to the hole. Some of the newer courses have as many as five tee stations, starting with beginner and advancing to expert. A general rule of thumb is that red tees are designated as the ladies tees; the white tees are for the average player; and the blue markings are for advanced or experienced golfers. Men who are beginners should generally tee off from the white tees.

Stand Off

When a player is teeing off, the others in the group should be standing together outside of the markers and off to the side to avoid being a distraction. Standing behind a player who's teeing off is akin to reading over someone's shoulder. It is rude and should not be done. If you have to ask if you're in the way, this too is a distraction. Use your common sense.

Keep It Down

Respect your fellow players. Talking, moving, or even standing close to a player while playing is poor judgment, not to mention potentially dangerous. You should refrain from whispering when a player is at the tee taking his or her practice swings and is ready to hit away. If, inadvertently, you have in some way disturbed the golfer during his or her swing, apologize. If you don't, the rest of the game will be filled with unnecessary tension.

On The Fairway
Cool Your Jets

Sometimes we're anxious to tee on the next hole as soon as we finish the previous one. You might even feel tempted to move along the group ahead of you while they're taking their second shot out on the fairway. Try to refrain from such behavior. The group ahead of you is most likely doing their best to move along too, so wait until they're out of ball-striking distance.

The Dirt on the Dirt

Proper play includes taking divots. In fact, if you're not taking them, you're probably not swinging very well. If you've just sent a chunk of real estate the size of Rhode Island into the next fairway, please pick it up and put it back. Replacing divots is one of the cornerstones of proper golf etiquette. Replacing divots is also essential to maintaining the course. Would you want to play on a course riddled with holes? Of course not. Chances are you wouldn't want to find a great shot of yours nestling in one either. Riding carts often provide a small shovel and a bucket of sand to assist you in repairing a divot. Please use it. If you happen to see another hole in the earth nearby, it's a good idea to fix that one too.

Carting About

If you're driving a cart on the course, do not pull up behind the player. Just as when standing at the tee to watch a fellow golfer swing, park alongside the golfer, but far enough away to avoid being a distraction.

Riding carts and pull carts should never encounter the green. The "carpet" is usually softer than the fairway and is very susceptible to damage. Pull carts, like shopping carts, can at times have minds of their own. Whether you rent a pull cart or use your own, make sure it's stable so your bag doesn't accidentally topple over, spilling your clubs and distracting a player's swing. Carts also tend to squeak, so check to make sure that an annoying sound is corrected by you or at the pro shop. Make sure your cart is generally in good shape, and that everything is tightened. If not properly maintained, cart wheels have been known to fly off and speed away from the golfer. If this happens, say on the second tee, you'll be lugging the wheel, the broken cart, and the bag for another seven holes.

Etiquette suggests placing your pull cart or riding cart right alongside where you will build your stance. This way, after you hit the ball, only a step or two is required to move on to your next shot, hence, keeping play moving.

Some golf courses make riding carts adhere to what's called the 90° rule. This means that carts must stay on the cart path and that the cart must be pulled up parallel to where the ball is. You cannot take the cart out onto the fairway to the ball. If you are unsure of which golf club to use, simply take more than one club to where your ball is. Having to go back and forth between the cart and the ball slows play tremendously.

If you are allowed unrestricted cart movement on the course, remember to turn off the cart before playing your shot. To that end, if you're sitting in the cart next to your fellow golfer, keep in mind that releasing the cart brake or throwing your clubs carelessly onto the cart causes a major distraction. Carts should also be parked to allow enough space for other carts to pass. Be aware of your actions.

How Many Practice Swings Are Allowed?

Practicing your swing is meant for the driving range, practice green, and lessons. It is not meant to be perfected on the golf course. In fact, except for the tee, taking practice swings when it was your turn to hit was not always allowed by the *Rules of Golf*. However, no such rule exists today, so technically there are no limits on how many practice swings you're allowed to take. For the most part, when it's your turn to hit, one or two should be enough. The longer you stand over your golf ball trying to set up the perfect swing, the tighter your body gets. Your mind starts to go around in circles and becomes deceptive. This results in slow, tedious play. In fact, when many pros step up to the ball, they do not take practice swings because they're fined if they slow up the game. Pros are limited to forty-five seconds to hit their shot from the time they reach their ball and the group in front of them is out of hitting distance. The key is to practice your swing while others are practicing theirs. When it's your turn, be ready and hit away, or as the case may be, putt away. If for some reason you find yourself taking more than two practice swings, make up for the time by moving more quickly on the course. If you're waiting to play because the group ahead of you is still in range, you can take as many practice swings as you like.

Watch What You Say

It's okay to point out the makeup of a hole. It's another thing to say something like "Watch out for the pond on your left, or the hazard on the right." It is rude to alert a fellow golfer about impending trouble and is never appreciated. If someone offers you unnecessary advice, be tactful and tell them that you appreciate their words, but would prefer not to be helped.

Umbrellas

If you're using an umbrella, remember that it can make a lot of noise when it is opened and closed. Be careful not to do either when a player is about to hit away.

When a Tie Occurs

If you find yourself in the same position away from the green with another golfer, decide among yourselves who should shoot first. The same goes for being on the green. See the Who Goes First section in the earlier part of this chapter if more than one player ties on a hole.

Taking Mulligans

Dropping a new ball after making a poor shot and not taking a penalty stroke is known as a Mulligan shot. Even though the Mulligan is occasionally taken during friendly play, it is illegal according to the *Rules of Golf*. The truth is Mulligans are a tremendous waste of time and are a major contributor to slow play. Some folks feel they deserve to take Mulligans every time they hit a poor shot, and the average golfer can hit many of them. Buck up and take responsibility for your game and your swing. If you feel the desperate need to hit the ball again, do so and take the stroke. This will soon cure your desire to take a Mulligan.

The Flying Clubs

We can all get frustrated on the course. Our rage can occasionally result in throwing our clubs. This is considered very bad form and you can injure your fellow players. If for some reason you find yourself hurling clubs, throw them forward; that way at least you can pick them up on the way to your ball and not slow the game down.

The Next Tee Box

As you approach the green by foot or riding cart, find the next tee box. It's a good idea to place your clubs or cart in that area and then arrive at the green. After everyone has holed out they can go straight to the next tee and tee off without having to go backward or sideways to find their carts and clubs, making for faster play.

If your ball isn't quite on the green, you can do two things: play the shot first then bring your clubs to the tee and return with your putter, or bring your clubs to the next tee and carry back your putter with the club you'll use to get onto the green. Be careful here: When two clubs are out of the bag, it's easy to lose one.

Playing Through

Playing through is allowing the group of golfers behind you to play ahead of you, and it is the right thing to do. However, if there were any situation in golf where generally civil folks lose it, this is it. Egos tend to clash when a good group of golfers catches up to an average group. The average group tends to feel inferior, while the better group tends to feel superior. Both are wrong. Letting faster players play through is the right thing to do, and those that are playing through should see it as a courtesy, not an entitlement.

Playing through can occur under a variety of circumstances. As stated, some foursomes play faster than others and can encounter a group at the tee with no one on the green in front of them. If twosomes are on the course, more than likely they're playing faster than foursomes and they would like to play through too. (Twosomes should pair up on the course whenever the opportunity presents itself.) A good place to play through is at the turn after the first nine holes have been played. Par threes, since they are shorter, are also a good place to play through. Under these circumstances the slower group should hit away, walk to the green, mark their balls, and indicate to the next group at the tee to begin.

Once a group is offered the opportunity to play through, they should say thank you and start to play. Any bags, tees, carts, or clubs belonging to the group that is letting the group behind them play through should be removed promptly. The group playing through should not take Mulligans. If a ball is lost, they should not take a long time to look for it.

If a course is particularly crowded and players are waiting to tee off at every hole, playing through will not speed things up, and therefore this courtesy should not be extended.

On The Green
Bags, Carts, Clubs

Before stepping on the green, leave your bags and carts outside on the skirt (fringe) of the green. On many occasions you can even take your bag or cart to the next tee and then bring your putter with you back to the green and proceed.

Take It Easy

The green is more fragile than the rest of the course. Please treat it so. Walk softly, never run. Remember to pick up your feet so as not to leave long, dragging cleat marks on the carpet.

Repairing Ball Marks

When a ball lands on a green it often makes a deep indentation known as a ball mark (this is not to be confused with marking your ball). This indentation needs to be repaired by the golfer who hit the ball. This is done with a golf tee or a ball repair tool. Depending on how the ball lands, it is sometimes difficult to spot this mark. Once it is discovered, take the repair tool or the tee and gently dig around the mark and manipulate it until it becomes even with the ground. Then take your putter and tap down on it to make sure it is firmly in place. If you see other ball marks on the green, repair them too, if time permits.

Tending the Pin

If you're playing without a caddie, the player with the ball closest to the cup tends the pin. Do not automatically remove the pin from the cup, as some may prefer it left in to help them locate the cup. If the pin is in the cup, remove it once the player putts. Do not wait for the ball to get near the cup. To tend the pin correctly, hold the shaft at arm's length. If it's windy, steady the flag. Also be aware of shadows. Make sure that your shadow is on the same side as the pin and the flag. Also make sure it's not on the putting line. If the player about to putt requests the pin be pulled, do so, remembering not to yank it out but to slowly turn it and pull it out gently. If no players want the flag stick in the cup, lay it down on the fringe or skirt of the green, not on the green itself.

The first person who holes out should be the one to retrieve and replace the flagstick after the last person sinks his or her ball. This allows the last person putting to move on to the next tee box without having to find the flag, pick it up, and place it back in the cup, which would obviously slow the game down.

Clubs

Refrain from letting clubs drop on the green. The "carpet" is very sensitive. Dropping a club on a green can cause unnecessary indentations that will need to be repaired.

The Line of Putt

Once the ball is on the green, there is an imaginary line that leads from the ball to the cup. Stepping on it is akin to punching the player in the face. Granted, you may at times feel like doing that, but hold off until you're in a boxing ring.

Holing Out

After sinking the ball into the cup, please remove it promptly. Although more than one ball can fit into the cup, it's bad form to leave it there. Many golfers are a superstitious lot and having more than one ball in a cup can set them off. Please respect them.

After everyone has holed out, place the flag carefully in the cup using two hands. This makes for less wear and tear on the cup, resulting in less maintenance for the course.

Support Club

You may have seen a pro on television after sinking a putt leaning on top of the putter grip for support while removing the ball from the cup. As much as you might like to copy the pros, avoid doing so in this case. Leaning on the putter pushes the carpet down around the tin, causing an unnecessary break and changing how a ball will roll on the green. Breaks on the green should only be created by the course architect or Mother Nature, not the player.

Scoring

Whether the last hole was good or bad, we all tend to be anxious to write down our scores and move on to the next tee. Refrain from placing your score on the card until you arrive there.

Bunkers
Entering and Exiting

Most bunkers are sand traps, sometimes referred to as "the beach." Bunkers however are a bit more fragile than the sand on the shore and should be treated as such. The lips and the rims of bunkers can be easily damaged, so enter and exit the sand trap from the low sides. Though you may be tempted, never jump in or climb up the wall of a bunker.

Where to Stand

If your fellow golfer is playing from the bunker onto the green, chances are some of you are already on the green. This is not an opportunity to line up and practice your putt. This is one of the tougher shots of the game, so there's no need to increase distractions. Stand out of view and let the person in the bunker take his or her shot.

Raking the Sand

Locate the rake before you enter the bunker. Once you have hit your sand shot, retrace your steps and pick up the rake outside of the bunker. Retrace your steps once more and rake backward to the fairway. Leaving the bunker in a different direction than you came in makes for more footsteps to be raked over, hence slowing down the game. Always leave the rake outside the bunker.

Postgame
After the Round

When the round ends, extend a warm handshake to your playing partners. This is especially good if you've had a poor round. It ends the game on a positive note. Whether your round was good or not so good, if you've taken a caddie with you, tip him or her well.

Rented Equipment

If you have rented equipment, clean off the clubheads and return the clubs to the pro shop or rental facility. If you have rented a cart, return it to where you picked it up or ask an attendant where it should be returned to.

Cleaning Up

Clean your golf shoes of grass and dirt after you have finished playing. Remove your shoes before entering the clubhouse, bathroom, or any dining facilities.

Take a shower once you've finished the round. If you're unable to do so, wash your face and hands. It'll make you feel good, and if you're having lunch, you'll look much more presentable.

Finally . . .

A good sport who's had a great round buys lunch.

Crash Goes the Window

Occasionally things might go badly for you on the course. Say you've just sliced your favorite dimpled projectile through a

window in a house on the edge of a course. Not only would the rules demand you take a stroke, but it would be poor etiquette for you to swing from the homeowner's dining room carpet. Technically, when a homeowner purchases a house at a golfing community, they assume the risk. They understand that there's a chance a ball may dent a shingle, crack a window, or wind up in a soufflée, and they'll have to pay for the repairs. Homeowners also recognize that they need to install some sort of protective device to stop such things from happening.

However, that's not always the case. There have been cases where course owners have had to pay for the damages. Etiquette-wise, the right thing to do is to buck up and come clean to the homeowner and offer to pay for replacement of the window.

Hole 4

Playing the Game

Playing Tips to Enhance Anyone's Game
A Word About the Grips

There are basically three ways to grip the club. The most popular is the Vardon grip, also known as the overlapping grip, in which the pinky overlaps the index finger. In the interlocking grip, the index finger locks in with the pinky. The baseball grip, in which the club is held like a baseball and the fingers don't overlap or interlock at all, is good for players with small hands. Some instructors swear by the grip; others feel students should grasp the club in the manner they feel comfortable with. Whatever style you choose, the grip should be firm but not tight. If you're holding it too tightly, then the rest of your body will be too stiff to swing properly.

Know Your Distance

At the driving range, learn how far you can hit with each club. This will help immensely when you're on the course. If there is one tip pros could teach all others, it's this one. The distances given in the chapter on equipment are for the average golfer; however, you may not be average. Once out on the links, you don't want to overshoot the green or come up short. You want to be able to set up your next shot properly. Not everyone is a power hitter like John Daly. Golf at every level is very much a game of finesse.

First Shot of the Day

When standing over the ball for your first shot of the day, relax. You don't want to kill the ball; you want to finesse the ball out onto the fairway.

Addressing the Ball

Golfers, like players of other sports, should stand in a ready position. That means standing with your feet shoulder-width apart, legs bent, and arms bent with your hands out front. Generally, the longer the shaft, the wider the stance. Place the sole of the club flat on the ground to find out how far you should stand with it. There's no need to stretch to swing the club or get in very close to it.

Keep Your Eye on the Ball

If you hit a ball poorly, it's going to immediately make your life a lot more difficult. Slow play is often attributed to golfers who don't keep their eye on the ball, then insist on looking for it for more than three minutes. As hard as it may be at times, keep your eyes on the ball until it stops rolling. Judge where it has landed and get there quickly. Look for a marker, a tree, bush, or anything to use as a reference point to help you locate your ball.

Marking a Ball Properly

Most golfers aren't exactly sure how to do this. Often, golfers try in one swoop to slip the marker under the ball, putting the marker precisely where they think the ball is and lifting the ball at the same time. To avoid making this common mistake, place the marker directly behind the ball, then lift it to clean or replace it. Put it back in front of the marker and remove the marker.

On the Score Card

Record how many putts you make on each green when you write down your total for each hole. This will help you get a fix on what you need to improve.

Hitting into and with the Wind

If you're hitting into the wind, take another club number down than you normally would use and swing smoothly (for example, if you would normally use a 5-iron, use a 4-iron instead). Hitting the ball too hard creates more backspin and may cause the ball to go too high, decreasing your distance and perhaps carrying your ball in the wrong direction.

For playing with the wind, you want to keep your ball down too. Hitting it high will make the ball much harder to control. It will go farther, but again, perhaps in the direction you don't want it to travel.

Swinging Away

The key to a good golf swing is to relax and swing easily; there's no need to crush the ball. Many new golfers simply try too hard. The backswing should come up slowly, winding the body tightly like a rubber band, then the downswing begins like a rubberband uncoiling. This is where the power comes from. As you come down, the big muscles in your shoulders, arms, and legs release, allowing the club to come down and strike the ball. This is not something that needs to be pushed. If you wind up correctly, the clubhead will do the rest when it strikes the ball. This is not to say that the club does all the work. It's simply an extension of your body, specifically, your hands. It's the power in your body that sends the ball to your goal.

Hit Down on the Ball

Hitting a golf ball is not scooping under it and lifting it into the air. One strikes a golf ball by hitting down on it. This pops the ball into the air and sends it either low or high, depending on what club one uses, how one addresses the ball, what kind of stance one has built, and most importantly, the quality of the golfer's swing.

THE GRIP

❶ The interlocking grip: The little finger on the right hand interlocks with the index finger of the left hand.

❷ The baseball or natural grip: All four fingers of both hands, lie on the club.

3a. Letting the club lie on the fingers of the right hand, place the little finger of the right hand so it lies on top and between the first and second fingers on the left hand.

③

The overlapping grip: The little finger on the right hand lies on top and between the index and second fingers on the left hand.

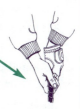

3b. With the heel of the left hand on top of the club, close your hand. The thumb and forefinger of the left hand should form a "V." The "V" should point to somewhere between your chin and right shoulder.

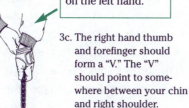

3c. The right hand thumb and forefinger should form a "V." The "V" should point to somewhere between your chin and right shoulder.

Playing the Lob Wedge

Focus on swinging the club in a sweeping motion. If you find yourself in the rough, trying to "dig" your ball out is detrimental. Let this high-lofted club do the work and remember to follow through completely.

The Pitch-and-Run Shot

This shot is good for when the pin is in back of the green, and is usually used from about 40 feet off the green. The goal is to get the ball rolling to the cup once it hits the green. Stand with your right foot farther from the target line than your left foot. This is known as a "closed" stance. On the backswing, bring the club approximately halfway up. On the downswing, concentrate on rotating your right arm over your left. This puts the toe of the club in the position to give the ball the proper spin. The ball sails up and lands on the green then runs to the pin.

Pitching the Ball into the Wind

The object here is to keep the ball low. A good way to do this is to place about two-thirds of your weight on your left foot and play the ball toward the back of your stance. With the clubhead a couple of inches behind your hands, take your backswing. Upon bringing your club down and through the ball, keep the follow-through short and your left wrist steady.

Pitching Tips from Seve Ballesteros

Whenever you need to hit a super-high, super-soft shot:

1. Choke down on the grip.
2. Stand as far away from the ball as is comfortably possible, with your feet in an open position.
3. Lower your hands dramatically.

4. Set the clubface wide open.
5. Swing down, trying to point the knuckles of your left hand skyward. This will help you slide the clubface underneath the ball and hit it super high.

Landing the Ball Soft on the Green from the Rough

Use a sand wedge and play the ball forward, using an open stance. Turn out the face of the club (opening up the face). Take your backswing and swing down on the ball. This movement will give the ball the proper spin so that it lands softly and will not run on the green.

Pitching from an Uphill Lie

Address the ball so that your body is at the same angle as the slope. This gives you a normal, flat lie. From here just swing away as you normally would.

Pitching from a Downhill Lie

In the case of the downhill lie, address the ball so it's closer to your back foot. This allows you to hit the ball correctly.

To Improve Your Chip Shot

A common fault in the chip shot is that golfers tend to stand too far away from the ball. To improve your shot, let your right arm bend a bit at the elbow. This will bring you closer to the ball, allowing you to hit better shots.

If Your Chip Shots Are Flying Off Line

Place two irons on the ground, parallel to each other and about a foot apart. Place your ball midway between the shafts. Address the ball as you normally would. Now, with your clubhead square, swing at the ball. If you find yourself striking the shafts, adjust your swing until you hit the ball without doing so.

If You're Hitting Your Chip Shots Too Long

Hitting long chip shots is often the result of lifting your left heel too high off the ground. This results in picking your club straight up and coming down too hard on the ball. Keep your left foot flat on the ground when executing your backswing.

Chipping Tip from Dave Pelz (the short-game guru)

"Good contact is crucial to good chipping because, after putting, this is the weakest swing in golf. Letting too much grass get between the clubface and the ball will sap that already limited power.

"To encourage crisp contact, place the ball two to three inches behind the center of your stance when you chip. Your stance should be very narrow—the heels only five to six inches apart—so the ball will be off your right (back) ankle. Since I suggest angling both feet toward the target to encourage a slight body turn through impact, the ball will appear to be behind your back foot. Now you can make a normal swing, and your club will descend on the ball with only a minimal amount of grass getting between them."

Preparing for the Bunker Shot

If your ball is in a bunker, take a practice shot or two outside the bunker. The rules of golf do not allow you to make any contact with the sand prior to hitting the ball out. Taking a practice shot in the sand incurs a penalty stroke. Once in the sand, plant your feet well. It's important not to lose your balance.

Hitting the Ball Out of the Sand Trap

When a ball is in the sand, it's the sand that takes the ball out. The way to execute this shot is to take a backswing about three-quarters of the way back, then downswing smoothly at about 75 percent of your normal speed. On the downswing, strike an area approximately two to four inches behind the ball, following through as you normally would, letting the sand lift the ball out. It should be noted that this applies to sand traps with soft sand. If the ball is resting on hard sand, then the ball must be struck.

How to Hit a Ball Sitting on Both the Sand and the Grass

In this case it's best to use a lob (third) wedge. Address the ball with the clubface open. Take the same backswing as you normally would on a bunker shot, but come down a bit harder, hitting a spot in the sand one to two inches behind the ball.

Hitting a Ball That's Up Against the Wall of a Sand Trap

In this situation, it's not always necessary to hit the ball out the side of the bunker. To execute this shot, open the clubface wide and choke down on the club. Take the backswing almost straight up, then on the downswing, while keeping the clubface open, strike the ball. This should pop the ball straight up and in front of you.

Hitting a Good Chip Shot

Hitting the ball with the bottom of your club, or topping the ball as it's often referred to, commonly happens during chip shots. The reason for this is that the chip is the crucial shot to get good placement on the green. What often happens in this situation is that during the backswing golfers tend to rise up, and this throws the whole swing off. The solution to this problem is to remember to keep your knees flexed throughout the entire swing. This will cure may chip ills, as you won't lift your body up too soon to see where you've hit the shot before you hit it.

Putting Properly

To putt a ball properly, one needs to keep the head and body still and lift the putter like a pendulum. Look at the hole from both sides before putting. This will help you understand which way the ball will break. For putting, only your arms and shoulders should be moving. To help you see if you're moving anything else, lean your head against a wall and perform your putting stroke.

Golf Swings—Common Problems and Remedies

Problem: Swinging too hard
- Attempting to initiate downswing with upper body.

Remedy: Initiate downswing with lower body.
- Swing at 80% effort.

Problem: Bending the left elbow
- Moving the clubhead back with the hands during the backswing.

Remedy: Don't move the left arm without moving shoulders.

Problem: Slice (curved flight from left to right of the golfer)
- Spin on the ball caused by hitting it with an open clubface. • Swing arc moving from

outside to inside during downswing. • Moving head to the right.

Remedy: Hit ball with more of a closed clubface. Rotate the forearms counterclockwise during downswing. • Initiate downswing with legs.

Problem: Hook (curved flight from right to left of the golfer)
• Moving head to left. • Closing clubface on contact with ball. • Swing arc moving from outside to inside during downswing with closed clubface.

Remedy: Swing around head and initiate downswing with the legs.
• Improper grip. Right hand too far under grip (strong grip); correct grip. • Moving past ball on impact due to improperly starting downswing with upper body; start down swing with lower body.

Hole 5

Mental Crosstraining

Professionals and amateurs agree that golf is a physical activity dominated by mental strategies. Unlike fast-paced sports where reflex, reaction, and quickness are often paramount to success, golf presents you with what often seems like an eternity between shots to think, rethink, and on occasion overthink your game. While other sports require a strategy versus an opponent, golf is a strategy against a course using one's own abilities.

The Modern Mental Approach: Practice and Visualization

The mental approach to the game has become the trademark of the new generation of golfers. Golfers are constantly trying to out-think, or at least keep pace with course designers who for years have been strategically laying out courses that test all aspects of a player's game.

To keep your mental game sharp, you need to practice not just your swing but visualizing your shot going where you want it to go. Visualization is a helpful technique in setting up and readying yourself for the next shot. It is a mental process whereby you visually take in what is around you and mentally create the image of your shot going from where you are standing (and about to hit the ball) to the destination you would like to see it land. Picture the shot leaving the ground and watch it travel as though you were watching a video tape of your upcoming shot.

The best way to make practice work for your game is to make the practice area as similar to the course as you can. If you focus on each shot from that bucket of 100 balls as your first and only drive for the hole, you will take more time and concern over making that shot count. Conversely, if you've practiced with the same mental approach, you can easily step up to that first tee, or any tee, and tell yourself it's the same as the practice range. Some golfers even visualize the driving range around their ball as they tee off.

Course Management

Course management is a way of planning your trip around a course. It refers to thinking your game through in much the same way a football coach maps out a strategy before the weekend match. Naturally, just as a coach will become more familiar with an opponent after a few meetings, the more you play a particular course, the more familiar you will become with the various ways to play that course. But, it's to your advantage to familiarize yourself with the strengths and shortcomings of your own game. Silly as that may sound, many golfers are still unaware of their own strengths and weaknesses, or unwilling to admit their shortcomings.

One of the keys to course management is knowing how far away you are from the pin. Markers notwithstanding, your particular angle to the pin matters, as do wind and obstacles. If you know how far away you are, know which club is best for your game, and determine the lie accurately, you'll be able to spend a few extra seconds lining up the clubface and mentally watching the ball go where you want it to land.

Setting Up Your Routine

To make the thought process and physical activity of hitting the ball merge together most effectively, it is to your advantage to try to set up a routine. A smooth routine will enable you to relax and take away a lot of anxiety.

Watch the pros and see how they go through the motions with ease, not pressure. You can follow a similar routine for each and every shot.

First, do not rush up to the ball, especially if you've just zoomed over via electric cart. If that's the case, walk away from the ball and back; make sure to slow yourself down. Electric carts

can speed up the round, but they also speed up your game and a hurried game is often not a well played one.

Stand behind the ball, judge the distance, look at the lie, and select a club. Pick a target a few feet in front of the ball, then select a desired target down the fairway. You might even imagine a line or clothesline connecting the two targets. Take a deep breath, take a practice swing or two, and imagine the ball going where you want it to go. Line up the clubface properly. Be aware of your body, knees, shoulders, and arms, as well as your hands on the club. Once everything feels comfortable, stop thinking and swing. The more you do a routine, the less you will have to think about it.

It's Still A Game, Honest It Is!

One of the most important things to keep in mind while putting together a routine and practicing your physical and mental approach to the game, is to remember that no matter how seriously you take it, golf is a game. When you have a bad day, enjoy the scenery; when you have a great hole, enjoy it, savor it. Golf is a game you can play for many years, but you may never master it. That's why you'll tell the tale of that one great round, or that ace, or another great moment on the course, time and time again.

Even the pros have their off days. That's why it's important to maintain a proper perspective, even while wrapping an unforgiving 9-iron around a tree. Golf can take you away from the real world. So why give yourself more stress and aggravation on the course?

To Think or not to Think? That Is the Question.

It's important to try to focus on each shot. Don't focus on the last three shots, or foresee the upcoming hole. Just as every pitcher makes each pitch count and every pass by a quarterback is consequential, so is your every shot. The more significant each shot is, the less of them you'll have to make.

You can overanalyze, think out every movement carefully, and be successful; or just step up to the ball and hit it. But, since golf requires so many different skills and abilities, your best chance of being consistently successful is to find a comfortable balance between the two approaches. First determine in which direction you lean: analytical or impulsive. If you can ascertain which side your personality leans toward, you can compensate on the course.

Are you the golfer who dares take the short cut through the trees, or the one who takes an extra shot and plays it safely around the dog leg? The daring, low-percentage shot can gain you a birdie or a ten, while the safe way yields a par or a bogey. The good course manager knows when to take the risk and when to play it safe. Factor in the way you've been hitting, the weather—especially the wind—and how much you have wagered on the hole. Sometimes your decision will be made for you by watching your partner's ball smash into a mighty oak and careen down a 200-foot ravine.

On the other hand, there are times you might want to try a new adventure. If you play the same course often, try playing it in different ways and see which works best for you. On an unfamiliar course you are probably best playing the safe route.

Hazards

Don't let hazards intimidate you. If you can't get around or over the hazard, sneak up on it. Sometimes playing it safe is better than playing it sandy.

Teeing the ball up on the left to avoid a hazard on the right is a great idea, and vice versa. However, if you know that you slice or hook more often than you hit the ball straight, take that into account. As for bunker shots, take some time to determine the depth of trouble you're in. Consider the lie of the ball, the amount of sand between the ball and the lip of the bunker, and the amount of green between the ball and the hole. If the ball is sitting up, you have a

much easier situation than if the ball is buried so deep that in the process of hitting it you may strike oil. Sometimes you can plan your escape, while other times the best thing to do is just get out, no matter how or where.

The Rain, The Wind, and Other Things

Weather is a factor in golf, as are well-watered fairways and greens. The mental approach also means taking into consideration every step you take that produces a sloshing sound. Wet grass will slow up any roll you might have anticipated. Keep the conditions in mind as you play, and don't let them frustrate you since they are out of your control.

The Approach

The approach we talk about here is not the approach to your shot, but to the course.

Since your tee-off time does not always allow for a leisurely approach to the course, you have to mentally develop a way of taking yourself from the outside world onto the golf course. How can you deliberately break from the real world and enter the world of golf?

Practical solutions include doing something relaxing just before going to the course or even in the car while driving to the course. For example, you may put on some relaxing music. Define what relaxes you and use a few minutes to focus on that particular area. Prior to relaxing you might clear your head by using a pad of paper and a pen, or a portable voice recorder to take down all the pertinent information that you are grappling with in other areas of your life. Note the office "TO DO" list or other plans, errands, or work-related activities and let the paper or tape recorder hold on to them so you can clear

your mind and focus on relaxing. Some golfers like to find a few minutes before going on the course to simply close their eyes and picture the course they are playing.

Relaxation gives you an acceptable transition into the golf mindset. Once you are there you can allow yourself to get psyched up and excited about your day on the course. A little apprehension about stepping up to the first tee is only normal. Even the pros have some butterflies in their stomach. Different players will reach different levels of excitement. Some players can play at their best when they are revved up, while others must be in a more tranquil state of mind.

It's also important that your expectations be reasonable. If you've just watched a PGA tournament on television on Saturday and you, an 18-handicap golfer, expect to go out and hit like the pros, you're setting yourself up for a major letdown. Know your skill level. If you play once a week, you won't be as proficient as the golfer who plays three or four times a week.

The same holds true for various clubs. If you've convinced yourself that you can't hit with a 3-wood, then you won't. If you tell yourself that just the way you became proficient with a 5- or a 7-iron, you will master the 3-wood, then you can learn to hit with it.

If you are in any type of competition, it should be one that is not over your head. Assess your handicap, which will help balance out the field, and play within your game.

The bottom line is to set up realistic expectations and not to create fears and myths about your game. If you believe it, you will make it a self-fulfilling prophecy. Be honest with yourself about your game, and you'll enjoy the game more and will probably improve because you'll know what level you are at and what level you are moving toward.

This is not to say that the average golfer should not venture onto a course that challenges low handicappers. You want to feel what it's like to play on the tougher courses.

Concentration

A downfall of many golfers is their inability to concentrate.

It's important to practice with distractions. They are part of the game and not the exception. The person who can study for

an exam with the radio on is used to having the distraction and has learned to tune it out. The golfer who becomes used to sounds and various distractions will be able to concentrate through them.

Concentrating is a matter of mind control and focus. If the scenery or other distractions are allowed to take away that focus, you will not be able to concentrate on your game. It's a matter of zeroing in on what you are doing and taking yourself away from everything else when necessary. It does not, however, mean playing in a trance. Concentration works best when it is applied at the right times.

Stress Management

We've all seen someone throw a club; sometimes we've been the club tosser ourselves. So what does one do to control anger on the course? Roll with the course, don't

fight with it. If you get frustrated easily, golf will drive you crazy. It's hard to maintain your composure on a day when every hole becomes a new and creative nightmare. If you can keep your cool and go with the flow, you'll be better off. That's easier said than done. There are occasions where you simply have to let it out, but try to keep them to a minimum. You'll play better if you approach the first shot after a bad one as the beginning of the rest of your game. You might even draw a line on the scorecard and tell yourself the day begins there. Give yourself a fresh start as many times as necessary, but keep the faith.

There are several manners in which to defuse anger while on the course. Walking off anger, trying to feel it leaving your body through your feet or your head may work. Humor is often a great way of diffusing anger. Joke about the shot, the game, the course, the cart, or the caddie, but filter your frustration through something funny.

If you need a place to vent anger, wash the ball in the ball washer with added vigor or carry an old rolled-up pair of socks or some similar benign, harmless object to pound or squeeze. The important thing is to diffuse your anger before your next shot, or it will take over your game. As anger builds, so does your score.

Breathing and Relaxation

It may sound odd, but it's important to remember to breathe before your shots. Too often, tension and anxiety result in short breaths or rapid breathing. A deep, cleansing breath is important for relaxation, for setting your sights on the desired goal, and for clearing the mind from other passing thoughts. It will also break your flow of bad breathing that will lead to bad shots. Taking in air will invigorate and wake you up.

Full relaxation exercises may not work well on the golf course, as there aren't too many places to lie down without someone running a cart over you. While watching others hit, you may try relaxing parts of the body that affect your game. Try tensing up and then relaxing the muscles in your arms and legs. Loosen up your neck and shoulder muscles and then relax your mind as well. One of the nicest aspects of golf is that the marvelous scenery that surrounds most courses can give you a nice diversion and take your mind away from everything else, even the pressures you are putting on yourself regarding your game.

Another relaxation technique is to picture something else on the course. Visualize something soothing, something that makes you smile. A brief daydream, particularly a tranquil or funny one, can relax you.

Jitters and Intimidation

Water jitters, first-hole jitters: golfers commonly are intimidated and develop performance anxiety in these areas. Water and other hazards are a challenge that one needs

to surmount to conquer the hole. You cannot hit a bad shot and get away with its rolling 150 yards to the green when a lake is in the way. And, whereas you may not have hit such a ground ball in years, the lake makes you think about it, just as standing on a fifty-sixth floor terrace makes you think about how high up you really are. And that is what hazards, bunkers, tree-lined fairways, and breaks in the green are all about. They make you use your skills, but more importantly, they make you think about the potential consequences.

The trick, and it's not easy, is to mentally remind yourself of the physical activity you have done so many times before. If you know you can hit the ball straight 200 yards, then the woods on either side of you should not be a factor. If you know you can comfortably hit a 9-iron and reach the green, then the water that sits between you and that green should not be a factor. The trick is to block out what interferes with your game. The anxiety is only valid if it is something that is not within your range as a golfer. If you cannot overcome the lake, then you must devise a strategy to sneak up on it and clear it on the second shot, or find a way through the rough around it.

First-hole jitters are a special, very common concern. The butterflies are in your stomach because you are just starting out. It is the first swing of the day, and you have people watching you. It's important that you take the first swings of the day on the practice tee and consider the first tee shot as your follow-up swing. Focus on the fact that you have already comfortably swung the club. As for the gallery, you know you'll do just fine on the second tee, where it's just you and your cohorts. So think of the first tee as the second tee, and that no one is around. Even top pros have first-hole jitters.

Hole 6

Anecdotes, Quotes, Jokes, and Trivia

Anecdotes

There's a story of a guest at the famed Augusta National golf course complaining to a caddie about all the gnats. "What are these things?" he asked the caddie. "They're Jackass flies," replied the caddie, "They're always found around jackasses." The angry guest quickly responded, "Are you calling me a jackass?" "No," replied the caddie "but apparently the flies can't seem to tell the difference."

Bob Hope once got a present of ninety golf balls with the words "Happy Birthday Bob" engraved on them. Said Hope, "Now when I hit a ball into the water, the fish will know who it belonged to."

○ ○ ○

Former Detroit Lions football star Alex Karras once hit a ball through a plate-glass window and into a dining room at a club where he was playing. Karras calmly walked over to a groundskeeper of the course and asked, "Is this room out of bounds?"

Ben Hogan once commented to the club president of Seminole that on that particular day the greens seemed slower than usual. The club president quipped back, "Well, if you didn't take so long to putt, the grass wouldn't have a chance to grow so long."

At Pebble Beach, in the 1965 Bing Crosby Tournament, an amateur named Matt Palacio hooked a drive on the eighteenth hole. As it headed toward the water he said, "Well, looks like only God can save that one." Just as he said it, the tide receded and the ball hit a rock and landed on the fairway. Palacio looked up and said, "Thank you."

There are those who are waiting for the ex-champion brat of tennis to take up golf someday. Apparently John McEnroe was quoted as saying, "Golf is artistic expression like ballet, except you can be a fat slob and still play golf." It will be interesting to see how easy it is for John to play through.

King Hassan II of Morocco loved the game of golf and had his own private course built. The 9-hole course had forty-three bunkers and the king could never seem to avoid landing in most of them. He called in golf pros who were experts at sand play to help him improve his game. After this failed, he did what any king would do and ordered the course changed and all forty-three bunkers filed-in with sod, proving once again, it's good to be the king.

President Grant supposedly took to the course with a friend because he heard golf was good exercise. After watching his friend struggle a bit on the course, he agreed that the game looked very much like it was good exercise. He then asked, "But what's that little white ball for?"

○ ○ ○

The mayor of Tallahassee, Florida, thought that because he was the mayor he could stroll onto the city-owned Hiliman Golf Course and play after the course was closed for the day. His off-hour practicing disturbed some, but he kept up his activity of practicing during the off hours. Finally, one evening, a maintenance worker asked the mayor to leave, and when he refused, he did what any good golf maintenance worker should do . . . he turned on the sprinklers. The mayor had the worker suspended, but the voters, outraged, backed the maintenance worker and eventually the mayor (and the employee) both apologized. The mayor promised his constituency he would not practice after hours again, and the maintenance worker returned to work and got his full pay.

Quotes

"You don't know what pressure is until you play for five bucks and you only have two in your pocket."

— *Lee Trevino*

🟢 🟢 🟢

"Building a golf course is like a tailor cutting a cloth. The routing is the cut of the cloth. If the routing is done well, the suit will fit. There may be some changes when you gain or

lose some weight, but adjustments can be made if the original cut is done properly."
— *Rees Jones on building and rebuilding courses.*

"Golf is a good walk spoiled."
— *Mark Twain*

"Some worship in churches, some in synagogues, some on golf courses."
— *Adlai Stevenson*

Describing his game: "I'd say I'm one under. One under a tree, one under a rock, one under a bush . . ."
— *former NHL goalie Gerry Cheevers*

Comparing golf to baseball: "In golf, when we hit a foul ball, we've got to go out there and play it."
— *Sam Snead*

"Golf is a game in which you yell fore, shoot six, and write down five."
— *unknown golfer . . . but a very profound one!*

"Golf isn't a sport, it's men in bad pants walking."
— *Rosie O'Donnell*

"Golf is a game in which one endeavors to control a ball with implements ill-adapted for the purposes."
— *Woodrow Wilson*

A golfer playing in Scotland once asked his caddie how long the hole was. The caddie replied, "It will take you three fine shots to get there in two."
— *Anonymous*

"Golf is the most fun you can have without taking your clothes off."
— *Chi Chi Rodriguez*

"Isn't it fun to go out on the course and lie in the sun?"

— *Bob Hope*

"If you are going to throw a club, it's important to throw it ahead of you, down the fairway, so you don't have to go back and pick it up."

— *Tommy Bolt, professional golfer*

"Golf is like a puzzle without an answer."

— *Gary Player*

"It is reasonable to assume that in the last five years Americans have lost, collectively, one billion golf balls. No other sporting endeavor can match that kind of dogged per-

severance in the face of such manifest futility."
— *Peter Andrews*

"I've seen courses built on landfills, and they've ruined a perfectly good garbage dump."
— *Jay Moorish, golf architect*

"If you hold a golfer close to your ear and listen like you would to a seashell, you'll hear an alibi."
— *Fred Beck*

"Most people play a fair game of golf . . . if you watch them."
— *Joey Adams*

"I must say, my pal Charley (Pride) hit some good woods . . . most of them were trees."
— *Glen Campbell*

"It's good sportsmanship not to pick up loose golf balls while they're still rolling."
— *Mark Twain*

"The Lord answers my prayers everywhere except on the golf course."
— *Reverend Billy Graham*

"Golf is a game of expletives not deleted."
— *Dr. Irving Gladstone*

"Golf is like love. One day you think you're too old, the next day you want to do it again."
— *Robert Di Vicenzo*

"I've done as much for golf as Truman Capote has done for Sumo wrestling."
— *Bob Hope*

Golf Humor—Optimist vs. Pessimist: A Quiz

Are you an optimist or a pessimist? Golf can easily help you to determine that personality trait.

1. A 200-yard drive on a 400-yard hole has you
   A. halfway to the green.
   B. halfway from the tee area.

    C. in the parking lot taking a chip shot from the hood of an '89 Camaro.
2. When you leave the course
    A. you feel that your game is improving.
    B. you seriously consider switching to tennis.
    C. the back nine is declared a federal disaster area.
3. The ball is sixty yards from the green, in thick rough, down a hill. You picture:
    A. the ball sailing onto the green.
    B. the ball rolling farther down the hill into an abyss.
    C. General Custer at his last stand.
4. There is a ravine in front of you.
    A. You are confident that you can clear it.
    B. You are packing up to head home.
    C. You consider throwing your club, bag, and partner in it.

5. If you play golf often, you look forward to someday:
   A. having a low handicap.
   B. having high blood pressure.
   C. having your head examined.

If you answered "A" to all of the above, you are the true golf optimist and despite your level of skill, you will always dream about playing at St. Andrews.

If you answered "B" to all of the above, you are the typical golf pessimist, but will keep on playing in hopes of that one great round.

If you answered "C" to all of the above, you might seriously consider tagging your golf clubs at your next garage sale.

Golf Humor— A "Real" Golfer Test

The true test of a real golfer is what he or she can endure on the course. Mother nature and keen architects have thrown many challenges at golfers around the world. Can you endure under any circumstance? Does a little wind, rain, or cold weather slow you down?

How Windy Is Windy?

1. Did your 30-yard chip shot to get onto the fifth green just whiz by the foursome walking off the seventeenth tee?
2. Has your putt already started toward the hole without you?
3. Is the glove that you thought you tucked into your back pocket now forty miles outside of downtown Duluth?
4. Did the pro shop just whiz by like the house in the *Wizard of Oz?*

How Rainy Is Rainy?

1. Is the course pro rounding up golfers in pairs?

2. Is the green now a water hazard?
3. Are salmon swimming up the fairway to spawn?
4. Did you caddie just hand you scuba gear?

How Cold Is Cold?

1. Has your ball frozen to the tee?
2. Have golfers climbed into your golf bag to stay warm?
3. Did the shaft on your four iron just snap upon impact?
4. Are a bunch of precocious ten-year-olds sledding from the elevated tee down to the fairway below?

How Hot Is Hot?

1. Are golfers taking their carts back to the clubhouse to have air conditioning installed?

2. Is the foursome ahead of you now skinny dipping in a water hazard?
3. Are players intentionally slicing balls close to the clubhouse so they can run inside and grab a cold beer?
4. Is the pin melting as you hold it waiting for others to putt?

A golf lover near Augusta stood outside his parked car en route to see the Masters tournament. A passing motorist stopped at a light and the golf lover asked, "Can you tell me how to get to the Masters?" Replied the passing motorist, "Practice, practice, practice."

The duffer swung and then said to his partner, "I'd move heaven and earth just to break a hundred." His partner replied, "You'd better work on heaven; you've already moved enough earth."

Two golfers were on the seventeenth green when one stopped for several moments to watch a funeral procession go by. "Why the interest in the procession?" asked one golfer. "She was the best wife I ever had," replied the other.

How can you tell an employee from the boss on a golf course? The employee is the one congratulating the other player on a 10. The employee is also the only player who can get a hole-in-one and say "Oops."

After hitting three balls into the water, the furious golfer flung the club into the water and screamed, "Damn caddie!"

"What did he do?" asked his partner.

"He gave me the wrong club," replied the irate golfer.

"What club was that?" inquired his partner.

The now more complacent golfer turned to his partner and replied, "Yours."

One player complained to his friend, "The way I slice and lose balls in the bushes, I should not only address the ball, I should put a return address on it as well."

The golfer asked his caddie, "Am I the worst golfer you've ever seen?" "I don't know yet," said the caddie. "This is my first day, but if you continue at this pace, I may never get to caddie again."

"Why are you so upset about your day on the course?"
"I kept my head down all day."
"Isn't that how you're supposed to play?"
"Sure, but while my head was down someone swiped my cart."

One golfer said to the other after watching a duffer digging up the course, "Should we swipe the ball for a joke?" "What joke?" said the other. "The way he plays he'll never know it's gone."

Said one golfer to his partner, "My wife left me because I told her I spent the whole day with a hooker."

The golfer asked his friend, "What should I give as a tip for the caddy?" Replied his pal, "Tell him to take up tennis."

The blushing bride rushed up to the first tee in her gown. The groom-to-be turned to her and said, "I told you, only if it rained."

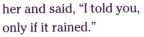

"You love golf so much you probably don't even remember our wedding day," said the wife.

"Sure I do," replied her husband. "It was the day after I birdied a 550-yard par five."

○ ○ ○

Two older women had just taken up the game. On the first tee, one of them hit a ball that sliced to the right, hit a tree, ricocheted off the roof of the clubhouse, bounced off a branch, careened off a rock, and rolled down a large hill onto the green and right into the cup. The second woman turned to her and said, "Why didn't you tell me you've been practicing?"

○ ○ ○

"You made one nice drive this afternoon."
"Which one?"
"The one in your car that got us to the course."

"How come your caddie keeps checking his watch?"

"What watch? The way I've been playing, I bought him a compass."

The golfer took a series of giant steps as he made his way to the green. "What's that all about," asked his partner? "Well," replied the golfer, "my wife told me that if I want to play tomorrow, it'll be over her dead body, so I'm practicing."

You know your game isn't improving when the course pro sets you up for a lesson . . . with the tennis instructor.

St. Peter and Moses were playing a game of golf. On the third tee St. Peter hit a shot that sliced way off course. Suddenly an angel swooped in, caught the ball, and flew it over to the hole, where she deposited the ball on the green. Moses turned to St. Peter and said, "C'mon Pete, not when we're playing for money."

The Golfer's Personality Index
Analyze Yourself (And Others) Through Golf

More than a game, golf is a way of life. It is an obsession to some and an addiction to others. It is a true test of what a person is made of, expressing their attributes, their disposition, and their personality traits and characteristics.

Much like the Minnesota Multiphasic Personality Inventory is used to try to determine an individual's personality, the Golfer's

Personality Index will do just that, based on nothing but the game, the courses, and the simple logic of illogic.

The system has been carefully devised by three weekend golfers who spent long hours doing painstaking research while watching a lopsided Sunday-night NFL game at a hotel resort bar on the outskirts of Trenton, New Jersey. Its accuracy is therefore unmatched by any other golf psychological personality profile known today.

Golfer's Personality Profile

Indicate your answer by circling one of the following:

1. *Doesn't describe me at all*
2. *Describes me somewhat*
3. *Describes me very much*
4. *Describes me to a tee*

1. When I slice my tee shot, I hear people laughing at me and making jokes.
   1   2   3   4

2. I suggest carrying our own clubs as a sign of bravado, but I really want to use an electric cart.
   1   2   3   4

3. After $500 worth of lessons my game is worse than it was before.
   1   2   3   4

4. I tell people who don't play with me that my drives go 250 yards, when at best they reach 200.
   1   2   3   4

5. I like playing new courses because they give me a host of opportunities to use new and innovative excuses.
   1   2   3   4

6a. (For men) I feel my putter is an extension of myself.
1   2   3   4

6b. (For women) Whenever I'm on the course I always meet some jerk who thinks his putter is an extension of himself.
1   2   3   4

7. I'm convinced my 3-iron is getting shorter.
1   2   3   4

8. I tell dirty jokes while walking down the fairway to relieve tension and take others' minds off the fact that my short game stinks.
1   2   3   4

9. I find the fact that my father-in-law has a membership in a country club with a

championship course to be his only redeeming feature.

1   2   3   4

10. The overlapping grip makes me hit like a trained chimp with a club in its hands.

1   2   3   4

If you scored between 10 and 15 points, you have no real idea of who you are on the course. You probably think St. Andrews is the patron saint of golf.

If you scored 16 to 25, you are getting familiar with the game. You recognize that the only thing a double green means to you is that you have two targets to miss.

If you scored between 26 and 35, welcome to the club. You are a lying, cheating, somewhat paranoid, typical golfer, who wasted money on lessons and would sell his or her in-laws for a shot at playing the Augusta National.

If you scored 36 to 40, you're trying to show off again!

Golf Trivia
Did You Know:

That only 17 percent of adult golfers maintain a handicap?

That the minimum depth in inches for a golf hole is four?

That the founder of the Walker Cup in 1922 was the grandfather of former President George Bush?

That only five pros have ever won the Grand Slam? Ben Hogan, Jack Nicklaus, Gary Player, Gene Sarazen, and Tiger Woods.

That a man by the name of Dr. Joseph Boydstone, in 1962, recorded eleven aces in one calendar year, three in one round?

That a man named Ollie Bowers, from South Carolina, played a record 9,756 holes of golf in one year (542 rounds)? Needless to say, his wife didn't see him often.

That Simon Chandler caddied at Augusta for over forty years?

That Byron Nelson captured his nineteenth victory of 1945 at Glen Garden, on the Fort Worth course, where he caddied as a boy?

That early America golfers wore tri-corner and wide-brimmed hats on the course until the commissioner's office determined that these hats were being used as target sites? They were ruled illegal for play on the links.

That a golfer named Lori Garbacz, apparently fed up with slow play, staged a protest by ordering a pizza between holes at the 1988 U.S. Open?

That at the 1989 U.S. Open in Oak Hill, four golfers hit aces on the same par-three hole in one day?

That two men, Simon Clough and Boris Janic, played 18-hole rounds of golf in five different countries in Europe in one day? "If it's the 2:30, we must be teeing off in Belgium."

That you can buy Grateful Dead golf products, including golf bags with dancing neon skeletons and head covers with the famed skull-and-roses design?

That in 1945 Byron Nelson scored an amazing eighteen PGA victories in one year? Ben Hogan made a run at that record the following year but fell five short at thirteen.

That in 1992 a six-year-old girl scored a hole-in-one at the Jimmy Clay Golf Course in Austin, Texas, on the eighty-five-yard par-three second hole?

That the Masters began in 1934 as a gathering of Bobby Jones's friends?

That there are two women golfers in the PGA Hall of Fame? They are Babe Zaharias and Patty Berg.

That Christmas Day is the easiest day to get a good tee-off time at Pebble Beach?

That Calamity Jane was the name of Bobby Jones's putter?

That golf is a $30 billion-a-year industry?

That 200 million golf balls are lost every year?

That if you play the third hole at Kittansett during low tide you can walk along the beach to the green? During high tide, however, good luck finding your ball.